Shattered

One man's journey
from childhood sexual abuse

Bill Harbeck

Holding onto Hope Ministries
www.holdingontohope.org
bill@holdingontohope.org
www.billharbeck.com
623-341-5792

PRESS

Shattered
One man's journey from childhood sexual abuse
by Bill Harbeck

Printed in the United States of America

ISBN 9781615791910

Unless otherwise indicated, Bible quotations are taken from
The New American Standard Bible®. Copyright
© 1960, 1962, 1963, 1968, 1971, 1972, 1973, 1975,
1977, 1995 by The Lockman Foundation. Used by
permission.
The Living Bible (TLB). Copyright © 1971 by Tyndale
House Foundation. Used by permission of Tyndale
House Publishers, Inc., Carol Stream, Illinois
60188.

Cover Graphic and Author Photo compliments of Jim & Mary Whitmer

www.xulonpress.com

To Jillian, my angel, who walks beside me in this journey and to Jaimee, Jeff, and Julee for their unending love.

Introduction

According to the U.S. Department of Health and Human Services, in 2004 there were 39 million survivors of childhood sexual abuse. They estimate there are three times as many that go unreported; which is one third of the U.S. population. Where is the outrage? Where are the cries for intervention from those in positions of power and authority? Why the silence?

Sexual abuse is a hideous crime. When perpetrated against children it stoops to the lowest level of evil. It robs them of their innocence. It scars them for life. It envelops their souls in toxic shame that renders them helpless to challenge those in positions of power in their lives, people they may need for survival.

Survivors retreat to the shadows and live in the darkness listening to lies about their own self worth. It is a silent killer. The very idea that someone would take advantage of an innocent child is hard to imagine. Conventional wisdom says something that dark should not be discussed in a public forum, thus allowing the silence to prevail. Abusers and survivors remain silent, fearing exposure and consequences. Survivors remain silent because the weight of shame in their hearts renders them powerless. Most often, the authorities in their lives have broken the innocence of trust. Speaking out and breaking that confidence goes against all they know.

Living in the world of silence has lasting consequences. Survivors develop coping strategies to counter the ongoing damage. Substance abuse, eating disorders, and violence are some of the symptoms generated by abuse. Abusers often become abusers themselves. Abuse damages the ability to communicate and trust others. It attacks survivors and convinces them that they are a failure. Striving to be accepted and valued by family, friends, and society they get caught in a vicious cycle of unrealistic expectations. Whether internal or external, when choices meet with failure, failure leads to dangerous behaviors, and dangerous behaviors to shame. Shame drives one to strive for good expectations again, and the endless cycle continues. If intervention and healing are absent, the damage will worsen over time.

Today there is a sinister abuser that is stealing away souls by the millions every minute. It reaches into every home and snatches away unsuspecting victims. The Internet, in just 15 short years, has become a weapon of mass destruction that destroys this world one soul at a time. The consequences of Internet pornography use and addiction are identical to the consequences for survivors of childhood sexual abuse. It is a 13.3 billion dollar business. There isn't much outcry against this from the leaders of this country. There isn't much attention given to this from the pulpits of churches. This, like traditional child abuse, remains silent in the public discourse.

Consider that each survivor lives in a family and community. The consequences for both family and community multiply exponentially. The plague needs to be exposed. It is time to offer hope to those who are suffering in silence.

Abuse is not a momentary affliction. It slowly eats away at the soul like cancer until it renders survivors incapable of feeling. Like cancer, the earlier the intervention, the better the chance for healing and survival. Healing begins when one faces the pain, chooses to confront the abuser, and intentionally strives to live in the light. It is an excruciating journey. It requires courage to step out and acknowledge what happened. It requires humility to recognize that living in silence is cowardly. It requires perseverance to endure the ups and downs of the recovery road. It requires the willingness to accept that you are truly wounded—it wasn't your fault, but you must forgive and in the end choose to survive.

This is my story, just one story of millions. Each survivor has his or her own unique version. Each survivor struggles on the journey. If you are a survivor, wherever you are on the road, hold on to the hope that there is comfort ahead. Hold on to the hope that you will once again find joy. Hold on to hope.

Chapter 1

Growing up in "Cleaverville"

I n 1955 television was making its way into the mainstream of American life. The fifties were a transition period from the devastation of the world wars to the cultural shift of the sixties and seventies. The new medium had the ability for the first time in history to communicate life in sound and moving pictures into homes. The evening news, entertainment, and sporting events were all within reach in the living room. Surely few in the general public imagined the power and influence this new technology would generate. At that time it didn't matter; the country was progressing rapidly and the feelings of prosperity and joy permeated the culture.

One television show that demonstrated this idealistic perception of America was the very popular program *Leave it to Beaver*; portraying two all-American boys, living in an all-American town, with all-American parents, attending an all-American school, with all-American friends and neighbors. Mom met Dad each day at the door after work in a house dress with the evening paper. Brothers Wally and Beaver would amble in the back door from school to fresh baked cookies. Beaver would share some crazy adventure from the day while Wally, the antagonistic brother, poked fun at Beaver's limited understanding of the ways of the world. The family sat down for the evening meal together and began to solve any problem at hand in a humorous way that always concluded with a smile and sense of security that all was well in this great country.

I grew up in a real Cleaver neighborhood in a suburb of Chicago, Illinois. Blocks of identical houses dotted our neighborhood filled with young families beginning to realize the American dream. And the kids, the kids were everywhere. Free time meant hanging outside with my friends. If I wasn't playing some sport in the street, I was riding my bike to the park. Five o'clock was dinnertime, and mom would yell out the window to come home. Mom never seemed to understand the bottom of the ninth, or tie scores, or the last play; it was dinnertime, and I better not be late. Some moms had bells they would ring signaling one had just a few minutes to get home, wash your hands, and be at the table.

Family dinner was as important as any activity, and being late was unacceptable. The dinner table was the place we talked about our day at school. It was where dad let me know his view on politics, religion, and sports. It was where mom schooled me on etiquette and the often-heard directive was offered: "I hope you don't behave like that when you are eating at your friend's house!"

There was lively discussion, laughter, and arguments. It was where we grew together. I never questioned the time or importance of the family dinner; it was life as I knew it.

After dinner, my sister and I would wash and dry dishes before anything else happened. In the summer those dishes did a lot of air drying, as getting back out to the street while there was still daylight was crucial. The neighborhood parents would emerge to their porches or walk along the street to exchange the latest news or just relax after a long day. The world I grew up in was cohesive, safe, carefree, and fun. An attitude of trust and civility blanketed the community and nurtured a sense of unity. It was "Cleaverville," just like the TV show that depicted the ideal community where nothing bad ever happened. We traveled through the fifties and early sixties without a care in the world. We didn't notice that the past century of ideas and inventions were changing the cultural landscape right before our very eyes.

My family mirrored the Cleaver ideal. Dad worked hard nine to five to provide for mom, my sister, and me. Mom was the typical housewife of the day, cleaning, cooking, and shuffling us around to school, piano lessons, and sports activities. Mom arranged special outings in the summer to amusement parks, zoos, and museums. She was always present and within reach but rarely intervened unless a neighborhood scuffle needed separation.

For the most part we kids in the neighborhood organized ourselves. Little league baseball was the only structured activity, which left us lots of free time to fill with our own activities. At our nearby neighborhood park we spent endless hours in the pool and on the fields, playing every sport we could think of. Bikes were our mode of transportation and we never gave checking in with mom a second thought. No one ever gave safety a second thought. My home was just one block from the bus stop. We would catch the bus and transfer to the elevated train in the city, which dropped us off at the front gate of Wrigley Field, the legendary home of the Chicago Cubs. At age twelve I would yell to mom, "I am going to the Cubs game". Mom would shout back over the vacuum cleaner, "be careful, and make sure you are home in time for dinner." There was no thought of danger, no fear of allowing me to ride the bus into the city. What a time to be a kid; a sunny day, $1.50 to sit in the grandstands, and $1.00 for a hot dog and coke. My boyhood heroes Ernie Banks, Billy Williams, Ron Santo, and Don Kessinger seemed bigger than life to me, and I always made it home in time for dinner.

Chapter 2

The Foundation

The church held a central role in most of the families who lived on our street. Church for my family was more than a Sunday event. We attended Sunday morning, Sunday evening, and Wednesday evening. Youth clubs met on Thursday evening, and we would attend regular week-long missionary conferences in the fall and spring. There were church picnics in the summer and many families gathered on other nights for fun. I earned eleven years of perfect attendance pins for not missing Sunday school. I learned at a very early age that attendance was not optional. Countless hours of training was poured into my mind through people I revered and trusted. They planted in me a core of beliefs and values I did not question and buried down deep in my soul.

I was a pretty normal kid and didn't realize at the time what the memorization and teaching really meant to my well-being. I remember one story in particular. Aunt Dorothy, as she was affectionately known by all the kids in the children's department, poured her life into every child every Sunday. At the annual Christmas program I was assigned a "piece" to recite in front of the entire church. Being just five years old, I was petrified and found a closet in the basement of the church to hide out. Just minutes before the program was to begin, Aunt Dorothy gently slid the door open and found me cowering behind some boxes. With tears in her eyes she scooped me up in her arms and whispered in my ear. "Billy, don't be afraid, I will be right there with you, and Jesus and I will be so proud to hear you say your piece." The love in her eyes and the compassion in her voice linger in my memory to this day.

Mom and Dad's commitment to the church, to service, and to others was lifelong. They lived out their devotion to each other without ever explaining it to me. They established an environment of security that protected my fragile soul. Looking back, the legalism was restrictive at times and a little stifling for a teenager, but it was always demonstrated in a spirit of love and concern for my well-being.

Without ever taking a class, or counseling, or seminars on proper parenting, mom and dad modeled for me a legacy that was present years later helping me with my children. What a gift. They had no idea through the years what wonderful grace they were showering on me with their unconditional love.

While the benefits of learning commitment to church and service to others was beneficial to my development, knowing the truth is all that really matters for me today. My earliest memories of Jesus were as Savior of my life. I learned in Sunday school how He walked on the water, how He healed the blind, and how He suffered on the cross. Mom and I prayed together one night and I asked the Savior of the world, the Creator of the universe to live in my heart. I had no idea what that meant at the time. I knew Mom and Dad had that, and I wanted it too. Many years later, after hundreds of books, thousands of services, programs, seminars, and groups, the intellectual truth can never match that moment with mom on our knees. The innocence of a little child and the promise of the perfect loving God cradled me to this very day. I will ever be holding on to the hope of seeing my Lord.

His death and resurrection, and the truth of His promise of life eternal are the hope for the entire world.

Chapter 3

Elementary School Days

I loved elementary school. The neighborhood Cleaver school was in walking distance from my house during nice weather, which in Chicago was anything over 30 degrees and not pouring rain. The school hadn't advanced to Kindergarten when I turned six, so I began in first grade. Mrs. Klein was the classic elementary teacher who cared as much for us as she did for the ABC's. I was very athletic and learned quickly that it carried great weight on the playground. If you could kick or throw a ball farther than the other guys you were picked first, or you did the picking. Winning on the playground meant instant status. Progressing through the grades I was able to make the basketball and baseball teams with ease, and even played a starring role. I wasn't a great student. It was more a case of application than ability. I fell in love with sports and couldn't get enough. I was able to manage grades and could have done better, but Mom and Dad never pressured me with high expectations.

I gained a lot of respect from teachers in elementary school because I was a happy kid willing to do anything a teacher asked. I volunteered to do errands and chores for teachers around school. My accomplishments in athletics and respect and reverence for teachers earned me a lot of extra privileges. I rarely missed a day of school; I had to be dying before Mom would let me stay home. I looked forward to every day as a typical happy Cleaver kid.

My elementary teachers affirmed daily what my parents and church taught. This country was founded by a brave group of people that had the courage to stand up for what they believed. The institution of government existed to provide protection for all Americans. We said the pledge of allegiance and sang God Bless America every morning.

On November 22, 1963, I was sitting in my third grade class, first row from the door, behind Sandra Mall, when the principal's voice came over the intercom. That was out of the ordinary, so we knew it must be something important. Through tears, Mr. Fenelli announced that President Kennedy had been shot. Mrs. Ballantine stopped class and asked us all to pray with her for the president's well being. I remember Mom meeting me at the door in tears after school telling me the president was dead. School was called off for three days while the country dealt with the shock. Television covered the tragedy around the clock, and Mom insisted my sister and I watch the funeral with her. How could something like this happen in this great country? It went against everything I was learning at home, church, and school. America mourned the loss for some time, but we are a resilient people and the transition of power went smoothly.

Life through the sixth grade was following the plan my parents intended. But it was 1967, the Beatles were shifting the musical landscape, the Vietnam War was escalating, and hippies were speaking of peace and love. The worldview my parents espoused was about to change dramatically.

Chapter 4

Shifting Sands

The parents of the fifties were the children of the Depression and two world wars. The country leaned to the conservative side as a whole. Judeo- Christian church values were tolerated and a significant part of the societal landscape. My parents are patriarchs of the baby boomer generation. It was important for them to transfer the values they learned from their parents to their children. In an era of prosperity and with the Depression still a memory, they worked hard to build the American dream of home and career and provide for their family all the luxuries they were denied as children. They preached hard work, family loyalty, and responsibility. I heard over and over from my grandmother about the desperation of the Depression years. She would throw her hands in the air in disgust and repeat, "these kids nowadays don't know how to save anything. A day is coming when they will understand what we went through."

As the fifties evolved, spurred on by a time of peace and prosperity never known in this country, the values of my grandparents began to erode under the pressure of material gain. Status was measured by whether you could keep up with the neighbors. Cars and airplanes made traveling affordable to more places in the world. Television provided new forms of entertainment. Radios played the latest music, which advanced the record player industry into homes.

Musicians, the pop cultural philosophers of the day, were now being heard on the radio, in the burger shops, and at home. By the end of the sixties technology had advanced to tape machines with little cassettes. No more huge vinyl records, now your music could travel with you—incredible. In no time the auto industry had tape players in cars right off the production line. It was quickly followed by Walkmans and then CD players, and today I-pods.

The rotary phone was replaced with a touch phone. It took only seconds to dial a number, and you could get more than one in your house. Pagers were able to access people in the mid-seventies. Captain James T Kirk of the Starship Enterprise, in the popular show *Star Trek* of the late sixties had a communication device where he just flipped up the cover and could talk to his ship or comrades instantly. No one imagined at the time that just ten years later there would be phones without cords, never mind phones that could fit in your pocket and have pictures on them. It was a time of euphoria, as the world literally changed before your very eyes.

One cannot underestimate the impact that television had on the changing culture. To this day, journalists point to the power television had on the 1962 presidential debates, arguing that Mr. Nixon's sweat beads on camera were a major factor in his losing the election.

Visual images instantly provided the viewer with connection to worldwide events, leaving nothing to the imagination. Every home had to have a TV. It was the new source of instant information. The nightly newscast started to replace the newspaper. Dinnertime was adjusted around Walter Cronkite.

Elvis Presley launched a new age in music radio and records. Crisscrossing the country doing state fairs and small town concerts, he rapidly emerged as the up-and-coming star of the rock and roll generation. When Presley appeared on the Ed Sullivan TV variety show, the" King" was launched like the rockets of the early sixties into worldwide hysteria. Not long after, the Beatles appeared on the Sullivan show. Instantly, their flamboyant style of music, their British flair, and their hair captivated the planet.

Television found its way into everything. Sporting events, movies, variety shows, and educational programs were covered live. The impact on the social structure of the family was immediate. Living rooms were rearranged. The den became the meeting place as the TV took center stage in the home. Status was measured by whether or not there was a color set in the house. My grandparents had a Zenith 680 color model complete with a remote control in 1967. Now that was status. It became a family ritual each New Year's Day to head to their house to see the Rose Parade in color.

In 1969 people gathered around storefronts, in department stores, and at home to witness the biggest historical event of all time. Neil Armstrong captured the entire world's attention as the first man to walk on the moon. Incredibly, live pictures were beamed back to earth and witnessed on television.

As early as 1975, videotape machines were developed for home use. The new machine, called a VCR, covered the top of the television, and with the touch of a finger your favorite movies were now in your living room. Even better, you could record your own movies and play them for family and friends' enjoyment—complete with sound and color pictures.

There is no denying that the sixties and seventies were a unique time in American history. With all of the improvements television brought to society, left unmonitored, it also possessed liabilities and potential for harm. Family discussion time disappeared and was replaced with entertainment and sporting events. The values and ideas promoted at dinner tables were now popularized by cartoons, newscasts, and sitcoms. TV became the babysitter, the information outlet, and the circus. The power of the new media was quickly recognized, and social planners used the airwaves to promote their ideas. Networks tested the lines of cultural acceptance with shows that crossed lines of modesty.

Today the rapid advance in technology has brought us personal media devices and computers that put the world at ones fingers instantly. Satellites provide worldwide contact. Ideas are spread across the Internet in seconds where it once took days, and weeks, or even years to communicate.

Ideas have consequences. In 1861 Charles Darwin promoted his ideas of naturalism in the public square, and it was not long before others adopted and adapted his ideas to the social structure of America. With the unsolicited assistance of Karl Marx, Sigmund Freud, John Dewey, and Julius Wellhausen, educational institutions systematically began teaching new ideas in this country with the intent to replace the tired old superstitious beliefs. These new ideas based on the superiority of man and the absolute truth of science became the accepted norm, and slowly nearly every institution of higher learning shifted its core to endorsing and teaching the new ideas. Dewey commented, "What can the traditional Sunday school, with its once-a-week teaching do to stop the onslaught of a steady dose of humanism?"

As the sixties and seventies unfolded, these changing ideas that were thoroughly planted in the previous two generations were unleashed on a conservative unsuspecting country. Not wishing to be left behind, mainline churches followed the wave of progressive thinking and exchanged their traditions for the allure of higher thinking. The conditions were right for the perfect storm.

Small earthquakes began to shatter the foundation of ideas. On college campuses, protests erupted directed at the "establishment". No one over thirty could be trusted anymore. Since man determined his own fate, the celebration of sex with anyone at any time replaced the archaic idea of monogamous marriage.

Drugs allowed one to go beyond simple thinking and launched the users into other dimensions of higher consciousness. Music became the voice of the philosophers of the age, combining radical ideas with heart-pounding rhythms. Woodstock culminated the changing paradigm and celebrated the new order with a weeklong orgy of sex, drugs, and rock and roll.

Violence highlighted the Democratic convention in Chicago in 1968. The proponents of the new thinking brought it to the streets. It was clear these ideas were not going to go away easily, if at all. The civil rights movement saw violent protests across the south and north as the clarity of prejudice and hate was uncovered for what it was.

The turbulent times cost this country two of its finest young leaders. The assassinations of Dr. King and Robert Kennedy were the fingerprint of the chaos of ideas that were swirling throughout the land.

Today the paradigm is entrenched in schools, government, the media, and churches and is the perceived core of ideas for the land. After decades of preparation through education and a turbulent time of revolution, technology provided the highway to entrench these ideas quickly. When the time was right all the ingredients came together, and in just twenty years centuries of accepted practice and value was swept away. The dust is still settling, and what continues to emerge is confusion, pain, and cynicism.

Chapter 5

Ideas Have Consequences

The traditional family way of life started eroding under the constant flow of cultural pressure. The steady rain of change loosened the foundation. The influx of technology, the allure of houses and land, and the temptations brightened by the switch in allegiance swept away the most significant of family values—loyalty.

The new worldview celebrated individual happiness above all else. Divorce emerged as the acceptable solution to any intrusion on one's freedom. Marriage, the foundation of a healthy secure society crumbled under the weight of ideas and influence. It fit. There are no rules anymore other than what makes you happy, so a lifelong commitment to one person is archaic thinking. Never mind the consequences to all parties involved. It's all about me. Today we observe the destruction the years of these ideas have produced. Over 50 percent of first-time marriages end in divorce. Innocent children are suffering the trauma of breakup and abuse. The selfish "all about me" philosophy is tearing away the soul of a nation.

Movies depicted the new age of intimacy, one that is about feelings and sex. Cohabitation replaced courting. Drugs enhanced intimacy. Norms were replaced with ideas, and all ideas deserve equal treatment. Opinions are sacred. Let's all live together in love and harmony. It was the wave of a new generation, a brave new world. Utopia was just around the bend.

In just a few short years the experiment began to elicit unpredicted consequences. Substance abuse raced to society damaging levels. New diseases transmitted through sexual contact emerged too rapidly to control. Technology provided a new source of illicit sexual activity for anyone that desired to view it, including vulnerable children. Churches and schools lost the high ground of moral superiority to the idea of political correctness and government authority. Institutions of higher learning became the bastion of liberal teaching.

Truth could no longer be known, so each person could decide the truth for themselves, to the current thinking that today truth cannot even be known. Houses and land, narcissism, and hedonism became the driving forces to happiness, where once the family and church held that privilege.

The single most destructive decision to the core of the country came in 1973 with the Roe vs. Wade decision to legalize abortion. In the stroke of a pen the leaders of the new paradigm declared that life is no longer sacred. A woman's right to choose trumps the Creator. Innocent unprotected life can be discarded simply because it is an inconvenience. Fifty million murders later we have lost the knowledge of the truth and sacredness of life. Once one abandons respect for life, anything goes. It has led to gender crisis, calls for euthanasia, embryonic destruction, and a prevailing disrespect for the value of human life.

In the late 50s Hugh Heffner embarked on publishing a magazine glorifying hedonism. Despite initial outrage, the magazine and ideas grew through the sixties and slowly tore down the cultural sense of modesty. In just fifty years the country progressed from movies to video tapes that could be viewed on the home television. Shortly after, DVDs, cell phones, and cable television made pornography accessible to anyone, anytime. Heffner's philosophy and desire to tear down accepted norms exploded in an industry that today generates 13.3 billion dollars a year. The ultimate attack has now come with the "Weapon of Mass Destruction", the Internet.

Today little children are exposed to pornography in the privacy of their home. Hard core pornography that was illegal forty years ago is now accessible twenty-four hours a day. Once again the paradigm shift comes with devastating consequences. Internet pornography is as sinister as any pedophile because in the secret world of the viewer, particularly a child, the intended design for proper maturing is hijacked and the damage to the soul is devastating. Today there are millions of wounded men and women walking through life like zombies, filled with shame and living in a silent hell, perceiving life as a hopeless existence.

The paradigm shift in the sixties loosened the centuries-old foundation of strong cultural values—values of family, country, and God. The structure is now teetering precariously on shifting sand. I lived through that turbulent time. I was thirteen years old in 1967. Being in the middle of the storm, I didn't recognize the changes all around me. I never imagined what was about to happen.

Chapter 6

A Wolf in Sheep's Clothing

My mom came from a large extended family with rural roots. My grandmother was one of eight children. Resources and experience taught them to be frugal. Saving rain water and paper bags was a regular and expected practice. Clothes were handed off to younger children and luxuries—are you kidding?—they were for the wealthy. Eating out for dinner was a once-a-year treat. Staying in a hotel was only in emergency situations or if you were on an extended trip without relatives in proximity. While my mom and dad didn't follow those practices religiously, it was clear that their upbringing had influenced their decision making and core values.

My mother's roots in central Illinois dated back to the early 1800s. My grandmother lived through the Depression. Families held together out of necessity. Loyalty to the clan was paramount to survival. One of the many unwritten rules was that anything that was part of the inner circle of the family remained in the inner circle. Bible values were lived out as a testament to neighbors and friends that the family was morally upright.

My parents modeled the same for us every day. It was expected that I would behave in the same way. Loyalty to the family trumped everything. Family behavior would demonstrate to everyone our commitment to God and the truth of the Bible above all else. No swearing or smoking in this godly family. I remember Grandma telling me once that she saw some new people in church and they weren't singing during the service. "They must not be Christians," she said.

Maintaining the image demanded our full attention. Others may choose to follow the ways of Satan, but not in this house. As the culture began to unravel right in front of us, it affirmed that those beliefs were right and true. As the onslaught escalated in the seventies, the family retreated to the safety of their home and the church erected walls, leaving the culture unchallenged.

Mom's rural conservative upbringing played out in her ideas of family hospitality. Her extended family remained in the Midwest, most located between central Illinois and Chicago. They remained close throughout the years and visited regularly, including a yearly family reunion when all of grandma's brothers and sisters brought their families to Champaign, Illinois for a day at a little country park.

The Depression and rural American tradition lent itself to homespun hospitality. When in town, it was expected that the family would provide relatives a place to stay. Mom's uncle Francis would visit us in Chicago occasionally, and she would always open our home to him. (From here on I will refer to him just as Uncle.)

Uncle was always entertaining. He had an infectious laugh and a repertoire of jokes that seemed unending to a kid and a quirky habit of using obscure vocabulary words to communicate. He was in excellent physical condition, not surprising since he was a career military man serving over thirty-five years in the Air Force. He loved to wrestle in the summer on the lawn. He would coax you into a simulated boxing match with jabs and uppercuts that were meant to bring a laugh but would occasionally connect.

Uncle had a fascination with cars and motorcycles. Every other year he would purchase a new car. It began with a 1954 baby blue Ford Thunderbird and progressed to the muscle cars of the mid sixties. His cars were always in immaculate condition. I remember being introduced to the set of polish rags he kept in the trunk. Any spots or dust was cleaned up instantly. Even though Midwest weather is always a challenge, his cars always had a showroom shine.

Prior to the explosion of NASCAR, there was USAC. Mom's uncle loved racing. From the small dirt tracks in the country to the speedways in Milwaukee and Indianapolis, he followed the circuit and talked about the drivers with me every visit. My dad took the three of us to a little track near our home in Chicago, and I was hooked. A night at the track with all the excitement, and most of all the noise and speed, still excite me today.

As I approached the teenage years, Mom began to invite Uncle to stay with us on all of his visits. They became more frequent and developed into a regular schedule in the late spring when the race season began in Wisconsin. Our home was a classic Chicago row house, three small bedrooms, a living room, small kitchen, one bathroom, and finished basement. My sister and I had our own rooms, and Mom thought nothing of having Uncle sleep with me in my room when in town. I had a double bed, and so there was no second thought as to where Uncle would sleep. I remember the first time we shared the room; his unending jokes went on forever. He would tickle me too, and I remember that night that he tickled me so long I was actually hurting from the laughter. The next morning at the breakfast table Mom asked, "What in the world was going on last night?" We glanced at each other and just started laughing.

In the spring of 1968 Uncle pulled into our driveway in a brand new yellow Ford Mustang fully decked out with a 429 cubic inch cobra jet engine, one of the original muscle cars.

All of our neighbors came out to admire the spotless shine and the sound of the powerful engine. Uncle popped the hood, and the sun glistened off the brilliant chrome headers. I was livin' large as my friends came by to see what all the fuss was about. I couldn't believe it when Uncle said in front of them all, "I've got tickets for the race in Milwaukee tomorrow right in the corner of the first turn." I was the envy of all my buddies and feeling pretty special.

Ninety miles seemed like nothing in that car. Parking near the track was always a challenge, especially finding a safe place for the Mustang. I remember so vividly stepping out of the car and hearing the thunder of the stock car engines doing warm up laps prior to the race. As we neared the track, the ground shook from the noise and I could smell the combination of burning rubber, gasoline, and concession stand barbecue smoke blending together into an unforgettable aroma. When all the pre-race pomp and circumstance ended, the crowd rose to its feet and the cars hurtled into the first turn battling each other for the lead. The sound was deafening, and my heart raced with excitement. A young up–and-coming driver named Mario Andretti battled the whole race with the master A.J. Foyt. The sounds, smells, and excitement of the day I will never forget. When the race ended, I just wanted to stay in the stands and relish the moment as long as possible.

The ninety mile trip home flew by as I recalled every moment of the day. I dreamed of the day we could do it all over again. We arrived at home in time for dinner and story-telling about the day that lasted well into the night. After dinner at the Dairy Queen, Uncle pulled out the race schedule and asked how many races I would like to see. I could not believe this; it was going to be the summer of my life.

My head was spinning from the events of the day. It was going to be hard to get to sleep for sure. When we finally settled in, Uncle Francis asked me, "Did you have fun today?"

"Are you kidding?" I responded. "This was one of the best days of my life; I can't wait until the next race."

Then out of nowhere came a question that haunts me to this day. "Bill," he asked, "Have you ever kissed anyone?" There was a long silence, and he asked again, "Have you ever kissed anyone?"

I fumbled for an answer and finally said, "Well, yea, my mom." He continued, "You know, when people have such great times together and they really care about each other, they seal it with a kiss. Would it be okay if I gave you a kiss?" Under those conditions, caught off guard and not wanting to appear ungrateful, I said "Yes." That single moment in time changed my life instantly forever.

The next morning we went to church then retreated home for the traditional Sunday Pot Roast dinner. Still recovering from the excitement of the day before, the discussion turned to all the possibilities for the summer. In two weeks we would go to the Indy-style race in Milwaukee. Then Uncle asked my mom and dad if it would be okay with them if I caught a bus down to the Air Force base where he was stationed, and he would show me around. The strange encounter from the night before was forgotten; it was as if it have never happened. All I knew was that this was going to be a great summer.

Waiting two weeks for the next race was difficult. When you are a kid, time seems to just drag by. I tried to keep busy with my friends in the neighborhood playing base-ball. Finally the weekend arrived, and we zipped up to the fairgrounds for the race. The Indy cars always came to Milwaukee the week following the Indianapolis 500. This was a whole new experience. These were open wheeled cars that were faster than the stock cars. The danger factor was much greater, which always raised the excitement level as the drivers battled with each other in such close quarters. It didn't matter to me what kind of cars, the thrill of being back at the track was enough.

We returned home quickly again in the new Mustang, making the traditional stop at Dairy Queen on the way. When we finally got to bed, Uncle once again asked me the question about kissing. I had just turned thirteen. The excitement of the race and the promise of more and exciting things was all I could think about, so when this question arose again, as awkward as it was, I agreed. I mean, my dad kissed me goodnight on the cheek, so what was the big deal? For me the allure of racing, and adventure overshadowed everything, so I agreed. I felt really uncomfortable and as soon as he stopped I quickly turned away and went to sleep.

The fourth of July meant a special USAC race in Milwaukee. Uncle came up early for this one so we could get an early start the day of the race. We secured our regular seats in the middle of turn one. It was a classic summer day, hot and humid, and I recall there were a whole bunch of wrecks on our end of the track. Jack Bousher owned a local car dealership and was the town favorite. I remember clearly the excitement when he won the race against notables like Fireball Roberts and Parnelli Jones.

We made it home in time to catch the fireworks display near our home. That night in bed, Uncle Francis asked me if I would like to come down to the base, where he said he would give me a tour. I would be able to get up close to all the planes and see the base in action. He also said there was a good chance we could go out in the country and I could drive his car. He quickly said that would have to remain as secret, because he was pretty sure my parents would not approve. We would check with my mom and dad in the morning to see if I could catch a bus down in a few weeks. If they agreed, Joe would pick me up at the bus station in Rantoul.

This was unbelievable. A chance to drive the mustang, visit the base, and see the planes, this was too good to be true. I agreed with great enthusiasm, and then the question came again: "Can I kiss you goodnight?" Awkwardly, I agreed, only this time things changed. He said, "Kissing is something you have to learn, so one day when you have a girlfriend and get married it won't be all new. It's like driving a car; you must start out slow and practice so you can become an expert."

Again, I felt really uncomfortable, but I wasn't in a position to say no, and I never anticipated what it was going to lead to. The first two times it was just a quick kiss on the lips. This time it was longer and more involved. I was being kissed by a man, and I didn't know what I was supposed to do. I allowed him to continue. I didn't resist, nor did I respond. I'm not sure how long it lasted. This time, though, something in my mind was telling me, *this isn't right. What would my parents say? What would my friends think? How would I explain this? This was too weird; there was no way I could tell anyone about this.* When it was over, Uncle said, "Now you must understand, when two people really care for each other, kissing is the bond that seals it, and it is a secret only they share. Other people could never understand."

I breathed a sigh of relief. It was over. I'll just never do that again, and I'll tell my mom that I would rather sleep on the living room couch when Uncle came to visit. Before I could turn over he said, "Oh, one more thing. Hugging and touching are another way of showing how much you care."

This time without even asking, he started hugging me and touching me. I tried to resist, I thought about jumping and running, I even thought about screaming out "stop," but I was frozen in the moment. When it was over I kept telling myself, "It isn't that bad, I can endure this. I'll just keep it a secret." I remained silent for the next thirty years.

The next morning was really awkward. Uncle's demeanor was exactly the same. I felt very confused. He was acting as if nothing happened, like a fifty-year-old man kissing a thirteen-year-old boy on the lips is no big deal. He raised the idea of me visiting the base. All I had to do was get to the bus station in Chicago and he could pick me up at the stop in Gilbert. Mom thought it was a great idea, and the two made arrangements for a date and bus fare. After lunch Uncle was saying good-bye to everyone, and he looked at me and said, "Don't forget about the ride in the country."

Mom overheard him and asked, "What ride?"

Uncle smiled at both of us and replied, "It's our secret."

"Oh, you guys and your cars," Mom chuckled. As Uncle drove away I thought, *here's your chance.* I could tell Mom what happened last night. But I couldn't get the words out. Besides, what would I say? What would my mom say? That could ruin everything. I had to keep it a secret, and Uncle Francis was holding all the cards. He knew exactly what he was doing, and I was a thirteen-year-old boy who didn't understand the game. I was an accomplice in his web of lies.

Chapter 7

The Road to Evil

S ummer was the best time of my life. No school, the endless hours of light, and the warm Midwest weather made growing up a gas. Playing baseball and hanging out with my friends on the block kept life simple. My best friend lived just eight doors down from me. We were inseparable in the summer. If I wasn't at Aldo's house, he was at mine. We spent hours at the park and had each other's back through everything. When we hit junior high we started exploring the world. We biked everywhere. I remember well the summer we discovered girls. There weren't any our age in the neighborhood, so we would bike to the park or their neighborhoods and just stand and talk on the streets. Girls were always in packs, and they were always laughing. It didn't matter to us, we liked the attention and the girls seemed to like it as well.

Three weeks had passed since Uncle was up for the race. Mom had made arrangements for me to take a Greyhound bus down to Rantoul to visit him at the Air Force base. The idea of sitting in a fighter jet cockpit and walking through a B-52 bomber erased all the confusion I felt about Uncle's advances. I was about to have the experience no other thirteen-year-old would ever get, not to mention the chance to drive too.

Mom put me on the bus—literally. It was very embarrassing, but considering that these days the thought of a thirteen-year-old traveling alone on a bus would not be considered, Mom was just showing genuine concern. She smiled, handed me a paper bag with a sandwich, some fruit, and cookies and gave me the usual speech about behavior and manners. Then she said, "Have a great time, Uncle Francis is going out of his way for you, be sure to thank him."

It was about a three-hour trip to Rantoul from Chicago. There were a number of service men on the bus making their way back to the base. It felt pretty special to be by myself. I tried hard to make it look like I wasn't just a thirteen-year-old kid. I chatted with a pilot about his life in the military and how I was interested in flying. He knew Uncle and talked very highly of him. "He's a good man" he said, "I am sure you will have a great time this weekend."

As planned, Uncle met me at the bus depot in Gilbert. We stopped for lunch on the way to his place, and he shared with me the plans for the weekend. "We will tour the base tomorrow," he said. "The Lt. approved it, and he will have a couple of the airmen show you around. Tonight, I have something special planned."

Central Illinois in August is a vast patchwork of green. Endless acres of corn and beans stretch to the horizon. Two-lane country roads wind for miles through the fields, with an occasional tractor providing the only noticeable traffic, making it a perfect place to learn to drive. We took off down one of those many country roads and proceeded to demonstrate what a 429 Cobra Jet engine could do. Uncle looked at me and said, "Hang on." He punched it, and within seconds we neared 100 mph. I was scared and excited at the same time. What a rush. Just when I was catching my breath, he pulled to the side of the road, jumped out and said, "Your turn." I had never been behind the wheel of a car that was moving. I hesitated, and Uncle said, "C'mon, there's nothing to it. I'll show you."

I sat behind the wheel and paused for a moment to take it all in. My heart started rushing when I grasped the leather steering wheel. No one used seat belts in those days. Uncle gave me a quick lesson. "D is for drive, P for park, and R for race." He chuckled when I gave him a look. "Gas is on the right, brake is on the left. Try not to hit anything," he said.

I eased out onto the road and slowly started to get a feel for the car. It didn't take long. I was overwhelmed by the power, and when uncle said, "hit it" I took off and found 70 miles an hour in just a few seconds. The road stretched for miles ahead, and I learned quickly the feel for a powerful machine and the thrill of speed I have never relinquished. Uncle let me drive down the road about ten miles before we turned around and headed back into town.

The 1968 mustang V-8 literally rumbled, and heads turned to admire the car and its power. Uncle pulled into the parking lot of the local airmen hangout and a few of the guys came over to admire the new machine. I felt pretty important talking about the power of the car and how I had just hit 80 miles per hour out in the country. As usual, Uncle popped the hood to show off the immaculate engine and the airmen all nodded their approval. "Just like Von" they said, "not a spot on her, even the wires are clean."

Inside, the bar was filled with Air Force guys playing pool and tossing back plenty of beers. Uncle introduced me to several of the guys and we hung out listening to stories and conquests for a few hours before heading home. What a day. A bus ride alone from home, my first drive in a muscle car, and hanging out in a bar with a bunch of service guys. Not many thirteen-year-olds I knew got a chance like that, and the weekend was just beginning.

Nineteen sixty-eight marked Uncle Francis's thirtieth year in the Air Force. As a veteran he was granted special privileges, including living off the base in private housing. He lived in a mobile home just a couple of miles from the base. I hadn't really thought about the fact that he had been a bachelor his whole life. I never asked him why he didn't get married. My mom told me he had a girlfriend when he was younger and she was the love of his life. Something went wrong and she broke everything off, and according to Mom, he never recovered.

Uncle had the reputation of being a miser. People would often comment about his meager life style and in the next breath chuckle about his hidden fortune. His mobile home was a two bedroom modest place that was meticulously kept. The military influence was obvious. He had a passion for cleanliness and order. Nothing was ever out of place.

He showed me where to place my things, my room, and the bathroom. He said go ahead and get ready for bed and then we'll have some ice cream. We talked about the day over a bowl of rocky road, and I found it hard to diminish my enthusiasm for all the fun. He shared a couple of his quirky jokes and we headed off to bed. I was barely sleeping when I felt him climbing in bed with me. I was a bit groggy, when without saying anything he began kissing me. This time it was forceful, and I remember being frightened by his aggression. Then it happened. He began touching me, and it became more intense by the minute. In a moment he was touching me everywhere, and I became very tense and uncomfortable. I was scared and wanted to cry out, but I couldn't.

Time stopped. It seemed to go on and on and then suddenly I had a flash, a tingling, and I felt dizzy and breathless. Finally he spoke. He asked me if I enjoyed it. I couldn't speak, I just nodded. He went back to his room. I tried to process what had happened, but it was all so confusing. I had experienced physical pleasure — something I had never felt before or even knew about. *Is this sex? I don't think I should be doing this,* I thought. I was very confused, and I prayed it wouldn't happen again.

Processing the whole experience was very difficult, and I had difficulty getting to sleep. In the morning Uncle again acted as if nothing happened. He just began sharing the plans for the day ahead. I started to treat it as just a normal part of the visits. It was clear it was not something to talk about, and I began to believe that everybody must do this. As Uncle shared with me the day ahead, the promise of a new day shifted my thoughts away from the mysterious experience of the night before and we were quickly on to a new adventure.

The day started out with a drive to Champaign to deliver a package for the Air Force. Then we headed back to the base for a tour of all the facilities and the best part—going through the planes. As promised, I was able to climb up into the seat of an F-9 fighter. It was hard to take it all in. The lieutenant explained all the capabilities of the plane, the instruments' purpose, and the cost of this amazing machine. Then he drove us over to the B-52, an enormous aircraft with four huge jet engines. We climbed up into the plane and learned all about its history and capabilities. I sat in the pilot seat as the lieutenant explained how the plane was being used in Vietnam.

I was overwhelmed by the entire experience on the base, but then the lieutenant escorted me and Uncle to another building on the base. He asked if I thought I would ever like to be a fighter pilot. As a young teenager, dreams are big and expectations even bigger. The lieutenant opened a door marked restricted and said, "Follow me, young man". He led me into a room where there was the cockpit of an F-9 fighter. "This is a simulator, Son," he said. "How would you like to fly it?" I turned to Uncle, and he had a smile on his face. I couldn't believe it. The lieutenant helped me into the pilot seat, buckled me in, gave me a helmet, and then he climbed in the seat behind. The canopy closed and I was in darkness with all the instruments lit up in front of me. After a quick lesson, we were flying. Once the plane was in the air he let me take the controls. I crashed six times. As we climbed out of the simulator, the Lieutenant asked if I enjoyed the experience. "Are you kidding?" I responded. "That was incredible."

"Well that's good," he said, "because if you were in a real plane you would have just cost the government about 60 million dollars."

I thanked the lieutenant several times for the tour and simulator experience. He smiled and said, "Civilians don't get this opportunity, but since Von is such a great man and leader on this base, we are happy to do it for him."

We stopped for dinner on the way home and talked at length about the whole day at the base. It was pretty late when we arrived home, but the ice cream tradition was never missed. We talked more about the simulator and my crashing ability. Then we headed off to bed. This night, Uncle didn't wait to come to my room. He climbed right into bed with me and it all began again. The incredible excitement of the day, turned into incredible confusion. I had been seduced into horrific behaviors with the promise of the things I enjoyed most in return. The White Witch of Narnia's Turkish delight had nothing on Uncle's enticements. He was patient in preparing me to be lured into his trap. I was thirteen, an unsuspecting innocent child. In a moment he took my innocence. He stole from me the chance to experience intimacy as it was designed. This was my introduction to sexual intimacy. I was told that this is what love is all about. I cried myself to sleep that night, and the lifelong journey of pain began.

Chapter 8

Learning to Cope

The next seven years were a blur. I was offered bigger and better enticements that my parents perceived as loving and kind. I rode my first motorcycle at age fourteen; a 650 Bonneville Triumph that was the standard of the day. I rode that bike all over central Illinois, and it sparked my love for motorcycles to this day.

Uncle purchased tickets to the Indianapolis 500 and I was able to attend and see Mario Andretti win his only 500 race. That trip to Indianapolis meant I had to bus down to Rantoul the day before the race. It was a calculated move, because it provided time for sexual contact. This time, the sexual behavior was expected. It was no longer a mystery, there wasn't any discussion, it began and it lasted longer and was more involved.

When I turned sixteen and had a driver's license Uncle would call and see if I wanted to drive down and make truck or exotic car deliveries. He had retired from the Air Force and taken a job as a delivery man for a local car dealer. It meant driving trucks or cars to the small rural towns in Illinois whose dealerships could not afford large inventories. It also meant driving big eighteen wheel tractor trailers. Once again it was the opportunity to do things few teenagers had the chance to experience. It was totally illegal. Nevertheless, it was just another one of the many things I could tell my friends, and it kept the allure going for Uncle. Each time I made the trip to Champaign; the abuse continued and became more frequent. I was expected to be available all night long.

All of the incredible gifts came with a price. In return for the cars, races, trucks, and planes, I was expected to provide favors without objection or disclosure. The first few years I remember the physical pleasure conflicting with the guilt feelings. The excitement of the activities outweighed the expectations of compliance to his advances. However, as I grew older and began to learn about the truth of human intimacy, the shame grew stronger and began to dominate my thoughts. I taught myself how to detach from the moments with him. I would think of anything I could to keep my mind off of what was happening. It was such a relief when it was all over. People ask me today, "Why did you go?" "Why didn't you just stay away?" It is hard to process if you haven't experienced it. If I changed my behavior or objected to all of the gifts and attention, I knew my parents would get suspicious. It seems awful to admit now, but the gifts were so great I just dismissed what was happening. I once tried to count all the times he molested me; I can only estimate that it was somewhere in the hundreds.

The shame and guilt took a toll on my personality. I was always an energetic happy kid. My father was an outgoing, fun-loving man who kept everyone smiling and laughing. I remember a time when I loved being that way. Going through high school I became angry and fearful of new situations. I resisted anything that would require meaningful conversation, and I withdrew to myself as much as possible. I chose not to make new friends, and I devoted myself to basketball. I avoided thinking about Uncle and the abuse unless he was around.

After being with him it would bother me for a couple of days, but I felt powerless to stop anything. I had let this go on for so long I felt I was at a point where I could never tell anyone. They would never understand. I was convinced they would think it was my fault. I must like it, so maybe I am the one that is wrong. All the thoughts and shame made me fearful of ever telling anyone. After a few days, I forgot what happened and went on with daily life. The change was gradual, and I am not convinced I even noticed nor understood what was happening. There were outbursts of sheer temper where I would slam the walls or scream at someone for the slightest intrusion. My parents dismissed all of it as age and hormones. Silence and seclusion slowly became the place I felt the most comfortable and most wanted to be.

I dreamed of a way I could still enjoy all the luxuries Uncle provided and somehow stop the physical contact. My parents loved the idea of all the outings and opportunities, and even later when I objected to going with him or to visit, Mom and Dad would say, "After all he has done for you, how can you just say no, or ignore his generosity? You owe him your respect."

So I held it all inside and I learned strategies to cover for the discomfort I felt and the confusion I wrestled with when I had to be with him. Silence was my safest place.

Every adolescent travels through the teen years searching for a place to belong. Having friends and being a part of a group is the most important part of development. At the time it is not a conscious pursuit, it's just life. Belonging and not being a nerd or geek is on every teen's mind. I was no different.

Since the fourth grade I had excelled in athletics, basketball in particular. I clearly remember trying out for the freshman squad. Ninety boys tried out for twenty-four positions. I was not from the local schools, so I was unknown and didn't have lots of friends. My coaches at the elementary and junior high level prepared me for the tryout, and I made the team easily and won a starting position from day one.

I gained instant status by making the squad and enjoyed being one of the popular kids on campus. Athletes were treated different, had immediate respect and, best of all, interest from the girls. My team was undefeated the first two seasons, and talk was all around about state championship possibilities the next two years.

Success meant hours in the spring and summer hanging out in the gym and interacting with teammates. My junior year came quickly and the team met all the expectations. The season was covered in the papers, there was unending talk of state titles, and every Friday night thousands came to see us play. I was able to play with incredible energy and desire and each time I was rewarded with the joy and satisfaction of success. I had a core group of friends and several admirers who made the entire school experience magic.

Away from the court my personality was different. I was quiet, withdrawn, moody, and aloof. There were frequent fits of anger if anything didn't go exactly as I expected. Any disagreements were met with a cynical sarcastic attitude. I was never wrong. I became antagonistic toward my parents—not in the normal adolescent way, but rather I was silent, detached, and unkind. It wasn't intentional. I didn't set out in the morning to be antagonistic or rebellious toward them, it just slowly emerged.

Every Sunday I would follow the routine at church and hear the sermons about obedience. I began to question the ideas and truths I had learned from my childhood. How do you know there really is a God? All the people in the church are hypocrites. I'm not sure I can believe this anymore. My friends at school have a lot of different ideas that seem like a lot more fun. I grew increasingly irritated with the constant attention toward goodness and right behavior. I knew in my head the truths and expectations, while my heart was growing anxious and troubled. I began to turn away from the church and questioned the truth in my mind. I kept up the image on the outside, while inside there was a tug of war. On Sunday I was the perfect Christian kid. Monday through Friday I was the shining star on campus. Some nights I cried myself to sleep with feelings of loneliness. Every night I would make up stories as I tried to get to sleep, stories of amazing accomplishments on the basketball court, stories where I was always the hero, and stories where I controlled everything.

My adoring father often tried to get me to speak, to tell him why I never wanted to talk about anything. "Son," he would say. "I can't help you if you won't talk. What's bothering you?"

"Nothing," I always responded, which most of the time I meant. So many times I wanted to tell him, I wanted him to know and the visits to stop. I always stopped just short; I could not hurt my parents that way. After all, it had been five years now; it was obviously my fault for letting this continue. I grew angry at my parents for not seeing and stopping this and angry at myself for not telling. I learned to live in many different boxes. I didn't think about the abuse box. I didn't spend much time in it unless I had to make a trip. As I got older, Uncle made fewer trips to Chicago and managed to get me to Champaign often. Then I really felt trapped, and wrestled often with the confusion.

I attribute my lack of social skills with girls in particular to the confusion caused by the abuse. As a sixteen-year-old with emerging hormones I was totally inept at understanding the proper behavior toward girls. I was petrified of just speaking to them. I couldn't look them in the eyes. I couldn't start a conversation, and if I had to speak the stupidest words came out. I took different routes around the halls to avoid having to say hi to two girls that showed an interest in me.

Basketball gave me a platform and visibility, and I could have had several girls on my arm at any time. Instead I hid in corners, went home as quickly as possible after school, and avoided any contact at all out of absolute fear. It wasn't a lack of interest, or desire, it was sheer fear. *What if I said something really stupid? What if they didn't like me? What if they did like me?* It was absolute panic, and it controlled each day and how I moved.

There was another problem: I knew about sexual feelings. While my parents never sat me down for the "sex" talk, I had a vivid understanding of sexual energy and feelings. I still wasn't quite sure of the biological procedures of procreation, but I knew quite a bit about the intensity of sexual feelings. The unsolicited passion I experienced translated into just that, passion. Raw feelings that were in no way connected to normal development. Here I was, sixteen years old, with normal developing hormones and interests that had only experienced abnormal direction.

A significant conflict began. I was strongly interested in girls; however, my interest was driven by a convoluted understanding of sexual feelings and the definition of love. Uncle told me repeatedly that people who were in love demonstrated it through sexual pleasures. While petrified of interacting with girls, I couldn't stop imagining what it would be like to be with one sexually. Instead of learning the protocols of dating and friendship, I was drawn to girls with purely sexual motives. Understanding a woman outside the sexual paradigm was something I was not taught, nor did I understand.

The church and my parents made it quite clear, repeatedly, that sex was only for marriage. Anything outside of that was reserved for hell. The confusion grew as I battled the virtues of church, the evil of abuse, and the intrigue of the opposite sex. The result was that I retreated more and more to the silence of my room and my fantasies about dating and sex.

There I sorted out the confusion to meet my own standards. There, no one could hurt me. There, I won every basketball game. There, every girl was in love with me. There, I was in charge of sex.

As if on cue, halfway through my sophomore year in high school I was introduced to pornography. A friend handed me an envelope at school one day and said, "Be careful with this." Inside were a dozen pictures of naked women. It was the first time I had seen anything like it, and to this day I can still see some of those images in my mind.

It was the early seventies, and Playboy and Penthouse magazines were around, but I had never seen one. It wasn't long before I learned how to get my hands on the magazines. Friends' dads had hidden stashes. Trash cans in the forest preserves were frequent places as well. I was curious, like anyone, and the allure turned into obsession. I welcomed any chance and opportunity to find and view anything I could get.

I had a job at the post office in the summers and found that the magazines were shipped in unsecured paper wrappers. I had easy access to them every month during the summer. The initial experience started me down the road, and as technology emerged I stayed right with it from magazines, to videos, DVDs and eventually the Internet. My confusing initiation to sexual feelings with Uncle was damaged further by the onslaught of pornographic images.

Pornography is more addicting and powerful than any drug. It pulls you into a silent world of fantasy where no one ever says no and women will do whatever you want whenever you want. Its sinister secret is that it takes more and more explicit stuff to satisfy the allure. Long after Uncle had stopped molesting me, I had pornography there to deliver the same feelings and pleasure I had experienced with him. Only now, I was with women, and in my mind that was acceptable. The confusion of sexual understanding and the availability of pornography blended together to steer me in all different directions.

At the age of sixteen, I began to search for an identity. I was experiencing serious sexual abuse at the hands of a family member. My lifelong attendance in church had indoctrinated me with what they all claimed was the truth. I excelled in athletics, which became my lifeline to healthy self-esteem. Eroticism became an all-consuming, distorted obsession that damaged my ability to learn and communicate with girls. I didn't understand at the time that this was not normal. I was just growing up. I didn't think I was different than anyone else. As if just being a teenager isn't enough, the numerous conflicts were molding me and slowly suffocating my soul.

Chapter 9

An Angel Unaware

I began attending church when I was ten days old. At the age of three we switched to another church, where I attended for the next twenty years. My father was the Sunday School President and for many years Mom was a faithful teacher in the toddler department. I had perfect attendance for eleven straight years. I never missed Awana clubs, the children's weekly program, and as I grew older was a stalwart member of the youth group. In other words, we were pillars in the church. I knew the language, the behaviors, and the expectations for Christian living.

One of the traditions at our church was the monthly Sunday evening pot luck supper. Everyone would bring a dish to pass, and you would enjoy the food and fellowship before the Sunday evening service. I was 10 years old and in line with my mother. Across the table filling her plate was a blond girl who caught my eye. Being only ten at the time, I sheepishly smiled across the table and she smiled back and said, "Hello, my name is Jill. What's your name?"

I don't recall if I even responded to her question. I had never seen her before and assumed she was just visiting. After dinner the service began upstairs, and low and behold, there was a family performing. A couple and their five children traveled the area singing and sharing with churches. Sure enough, there was the little blond girl who said "hi" to me right in the front of the group. Not only was she cute, she could sing. I mean really sing. I was smitten, if you can be smitten at age 10. I remember clearly on the way home my mom asking what I thought of the family. "Great singers," I responded, "And the blond girl was amazing. I think she said her name is Jill."

Several years later I was sitting in church waiting for Sunday school to start and in walked the little blond girl, who wasn't little anymore. Her father had accepted a position in our church with the music staff and they were now members. This time on the ride home, I told my mom she is the girl I would like to marry someday. Mom chuckled and responded, "They are a good Christian family, but let's not worry about marriage just yet. You are only thirteen."

We began a Sunday-only friendship. It was rather competitive at first. She loved to win and took great pride in beating me in Bible verse contests before Sunday school started each week. She was vivacious, winsome, and talked endlessly.

Sunday school began with some welcome exercises with the entire group, followed by instruction time in smaller groups. Between Sunday school and the morning service there was fifteen minutes each week to interact. I looked forward to every Sunday and the fifteen minutes hanging out near her.

The summer of 1968 brought with it the realization that there was a year difference in our ages. This presented a problem. When school began she would head off to another group on Sunday mornings. More critical, being seen speaking to an 8th grader was socially unacceptable. That one year barrier at that time in my life was like the Great Wall of China. I recognized the obvious. There are some rules you just don't mess with. But, a friendship had begun.

Unfortunately, it was the same time that the abuse began. My brief introduction into the world of courting was cut short. The opportunity to develop a "normal" courting relationship ended. What was beginning as a normal, acceptable friendship was cut short by age and abuse.

My neighborhood school district was small, and so the elementary school I attended was kindergarten through eighth grade. Many of the other school districts surrounding us had a separate seventh and eighth grade junior high. What was sacrificed in size and resources our little school made up for with a cozy family atmosphere.

I was not sexually savvy in eighth grade. I was not clear about the biological system of reproduction. When the molesting began the previous spring I became more curious and hunted for books or magazines that would enlighten me. I vividly recall finding a biological manual complete with anatomy diagrams and explanations. Wow, that was an eye opener.

Winter in the Midwest eliminated the summer outdoor activities, which meant I didn't see Uncle Francis very often. All my other activities continued that year and I graduated from eighth grade in June anticipating high school in the fall. It also meant I could renew my friendship with Jill. I would be able to see her every week on Sunday and in the regular Friday night youth group meetings, not to mention other special outings.

There were many times that summer that I was able to be with Jill, and once again her winsome personality captivated me. Picnics, amusement parks, baseball games were all secondary to the chance to be near her. We moved as a youth group, which really didn't matter. She showed an interest in me and she was so much fun to be around.

Late in the summer I mentioned to my uncle that I had a girlfriend—at least in my mind she was. I wanted to see what he would say. Uncle made a statement to me that I heard, but it didn't sink in at the time. He said, "When you get a steady girlfriend someday, and you decide to get married, you will belong to her only."

A steady girlfriend? Married? I was fourteen. According to my mom I wasn't supposed to even be thinking about dating until I was sixteen. I was sexually active at age thirteen through no choice of my own. In reality, I was sexually confused. All I knew was that I wanted to be near her as much as possible.

Sunday morning two weeks before school started in the fall, devastating news came. Jill told me her father had decided she should attend a private school in Iowa the coming year. What? How could this be? I was finally in high school and we could see each other a couple times a week. This was terrible. She liked me. The day I watched her drive away melted me to the core. At this very crucial time in my life, the person I wanted to be near was going away. I experienced loneliness for the first time.

The first few weeks in high school were beyond traumatic. The elementary school I left had only 100 students in our graduating class. Now there were four thousand walking the halls of a huge place, and I only knew a few from my own neighborhood. I developed stomach issues that my parents and doctor passed off to nerves. True, I was very nervous about trying out for the basketball team, but it was more than nerves. They didn't understand how much Jill being gone affected me. They didn't understand how much I didn't want to see Uncle Joe anymore. What he was doing had to stop; I had a girlfriend now.

Strangely, at school, I was afraid of the girls and starting up friendships. Jill and I had grown up together. Now she was gone. Whom could I talk to, and about what? Being alone became the best and safest place to be. The problems you can't control and can't share are best left inside. If you don't talk about them maybe they will go away. I couldn't talk to anyone about Uncle. I couldn't call Jill. I started living in my own little safe world, where my greatest fear was that I had lost Jill.

The annual Halloween party came that fall at church, and I decided to go. When I arrived I couldn't believe it. There she was, dressed like a little Dutch girl complete with blonde pig tail braids. She had come home from school for the weekend and heard about the party at church. I stood in the corner as she interacted with everyone.

She had the most incredible personality. She brought the best out in everyone. I feared she was no longer interested in our friendship so I avoided her as best I could. What if she comes and talks to me? What will I say? She is so much better than me. As I was playing failure over and over in my head, I lost sight of her.

All of a sudden she tapped me on the shoulder and smiled at me with her infectious smile and said, "Hi, I've been looking for you. Follow me." She proceeded to lead me over to the apple dunking tank. She turned and said, "Watch this." She threw an apple in the air, believing she could catch it in her mouth like a marshmallow. I stared in amazement as the apple came crashing down on her face. I could not believe what I had just witnessed. Blood was dripping from her teeth as her lips began to swell. I was smitten again. This girl was fearless, or maybe just a little crazy. But she was free. She was living life to the fullest, offering no negative words, all the time encouraging, funny, compassionate, and beautiful. She made me feel excited about everything.

The rest of the evening went by so quickly, and I didn't sleep all night thinking about the apple and the fact that she wanted to hang out with me. I saw her again on Sunday morning. She had to leave for school right after church, and once again watching her drive away tore at my heart as I withdrew into myself. I became quiet and distanced and started losing interest in church. That would never be an option with my parents. My complicit attitude aside, without Jill there, it lacked energy. She was the attraction now, not the church.

I wouldn't see her again until the two week Christmas vacation. The first week in November I made the basketball team. I was relieved and rejuvenated, and it took the edge off Jill being gone. Missing her was a little easier now that I had practice and the team to focus on. I didn't understand for many years what began to emerge in my behavior. It was as if a dark would descended over my mind without warning. My mood would change instantly, without provocation or control. I lashed out at my sister over little things that never upset me before. I responded to my parents with short, sarcastic, disrespectful quips, or not at all. Mom and Dad confronted me occasionally about my deteriorating attitude. "Where is all this coming from?" they would ask. I responded with the typical teenage mantra: "I don't know."

I retreated to my bedroom anytime I was home and resisted going to church and youth group as much as possible. As Christmas drew near, I had grown so angry I didn't want to attend the Christmas services because I knew Jill would be there. I just didn't want to see her. Part of me couldn't stand the idea of not seeing her and part of me didn't want to see her at all. We attended different services that Christmas, so it appeared I would not see her at all over the break. It angered me, and yet I did nothing to try to connect. There was a constant battle going on in my head that didn't make sense. How could you like someone and not like someone at the same time?

The New Year's Eve service at church lasted from 6 p.m. until midnight. It would be really hard to avoid her the whole evening. I asked my parents if I could stay home. Of course they said no. I was able to avoid her the whole evening, when just around midnight she came running to me. "Where have you been? I have been looking all over for you. Are you mad at me? I wanted to tell you Merry Christmas and Happy New Year."

Instead, I said, "Thanks" without a smile. Part of me was saying, *stay away from me. If you only knew the real me you would never talk to me, never want anything to do with me.* The other part of me was melting inside. I wanted so much to talk with her and laugh with her and enjoy being around her, but something was holding me back, so I didn't say anything.

She asked, "What's wrong? Why do you look so sad?" I just nodded and quietly responded, "I am fine."

"I'll be back for Easter," she said. "Can we talk then?"

"Sure, I suppose" I responded without any visible emotion. As she walked away, once again, my heart was running with her.

I didn't see her at Easter; in fact I didn't see her again until the following summer. She was home, and it would mean seeing her often at church and youth outings. That summer started a long pattern of bizarre dysfunctional behavior that lasted for years. Her competitive nature viewed me as a challenge. She decided that she would do everything within her power to make me talk, smile, and laugh every time she saw me. It became her mission. She pursued, and pursued, and pursued as I resisted. However, I craved the attention, I desperately wanted her to keep pursuing, yet my response was often unkind and confusing. I would literally remain silent until I could sense she might go away. Then I would respond just enough to keep her pursuing. It was working great until the fall rolled around and it was time for school.

Unfortunately she had to have surgery, and her parents decided it best that she remain home for the fall semester. I was thrilled. I would see her all the time now, and we could continue this crazy courtship game I had engineered.

Our friendship continued to grow despite my abnormal behavior. For some crazy reason, she ignored my moods, my anger, and silence. Adolescent hormones began to emerge, and I remember experimenting with physical affection. I was in the midst of confusion. On the one hand, the abuse had short-circuited my understanding of intimacy and proper behavior. But on the other hand, I was developing a physical attraction to my only friend. Communicating, enjoying life, and sharing experiences—in other words, developing a healthy relationship—was colliding with the inappropriate sexual feelings I had experienced. I thought sexual feelings and involvement was what I was to be striving for. That's what I had been told by my abuser. When you really love someone this is what you do.

I was playing a game with her on the outside while on the inside I was in complete turmoil. She had no way of knowing what was going on in my head. All she knew was that I was a quiet, cautious, boy that she was attracted to. Her compassionate heart kept pursuing. I didn't have to say anything. She had the ability to make me and everyone happy. I could keep my secret and have all the benefits of a friend. The next two years saw us drawing closer and closer despite the dysfunctional relationship we shared.

Being a year older than me, Jill graduated high school and began nursing school while I was in my last year of high school. We spent a lot of time together, and my aggressive physical behavior was causing a strain on our friendship. I believed that physical touch was how you showed interest for the one you really loved. I never communicated feelings or desires. I never communicated period. Jill had to draw everything out of me. We grew closer because I needed her attention without having to do anything and she was determined to fix me, even though she had no idea what she was dealing with.

My senior year became a pivotal point. The team was moving through the year with great success. My teammates and I were standing tall on the campus and community. Jill and I were totally steady, and it seemed to be a given to all who saw and knew us that marriage was just when, not if. However, Uncle Joe continued to pursue me, and three times that year he insisted I come down for visits. On the drive I plotted ways to avoid the contact. One trip I reserved a hotel room nearby and planned to just hold over there for the weekend and then head home. It was a great plan, except for the truth that I would have to explain to everyone why I didn't show up. Uncle would certainly have called my parents when I failed to arrive. Then it would mean either lying about my whereabouts, or revealing the truth. The noose got tighter and tighter with each trip. Each time I resisted, my parents responded with, "After all he's done for you, there is no way you are not going." On the trips down I boiled inside with anger, and on the ride home it spilled over into fits of rage. I remember banging the steering wheel and screaming in the empty car. For miles, tears just flowed as I tried to find a solution. Each time after the three hour ride, I retreated to my silent world and my secret.

In March that year, the foundation of my self-esteem crumbled. For the second year in a row we lost in the state basketball tournament in the quarterfinals. The loss crushed me. This time, I saw myself as the loser, not the team. People would never cheer for me again. I was finished. No more basketball. I had not prepared in any way for college. No one called with a scholarship offer. What now?

June came quickly that spring, and I graduated. It was a great day that I recall with happy memories. Lest one think that I lived in the world of despair 24/7, I had the ability to compartmentalize my life and activities and demonstrate appropriate joy and excitement when necessary, or when I chose to leave the dark side. The summer held a lot of promise for new adventure, and I remember clearly the excitement of a new beginning. Starting in junior high I had a paper route. I saved every penny from that job, over six years, and the day

I turned eighteen, I bought a brand new motorcycle. I could not wait to get out on the road and enjoy the freedom. The best part of it all was that Jill and I had the whole summer to be together.

Earlier in the spring, after the coach called several times, I chose to attend nearby Wheaton College in the fall. I had not distinguished myself academically, and that was an issue for prestigious Wheaton. Coach Pfund was a legend at the college and assured me that the denial letter I received from the admissions office was sent in error. "Never mind that letter Bill" he said over the phone. "We are looking forward to having you at school in the fall and on the basketball team this winter." It all sounded great to me. Jill was attending nursing school near her home, so it meant we could be in close contact that year. I liked the prospects for the new beginning.

Chapter 10

Welcome to Wheaton

Wheaton College is located just thirty miles west of Chicago, Illinois. Traveling time from my house was about forty-five minutes. It wasn't like going out of state, but it was just far enough to separate me from my parents. From day one, my fundamental roots were challenged and my eyes were opened to many new ways of thinking. I didn't see Jill as much as I had anticipated, and I didn't apply myself in the classroom the first semester. I thought I was just going to play basketball and school would take care of itself. That's the way it had been in high school. After a stern warning from one of the upperclassmen and a mid-term wake-up call about something called eligibility, I learned quickly about the rigors of college academics. I dug in quickly and realized that I had missed many opportunities in high school as a student. Call it immaturity, lack of parental pressure, or even the dysfunction of abuse, whatever the root cause; I discovered that I could excel in the classroom if I applied myself. Years later I found reading, and it excites me to this day.

My high school basketball experience was the tether line that kept the consequences of the abuse in check. The winning provided the sense of worth I needed to combat the fear of failure that was developing in my soul. Shame is a hideous weapon I believe Satan uses to drive one into submission. Not guilt that God designed for man to check himself and learn of repentance and forgiveness because of our inborn sin, but rather toxic shame that tears apart the soul. It's shame that lies to your heart and tells you that you are a worthless, dirty failure. It's shame that produces the anger that spews out at unexpected moments with no warning. It's shame that damages your soul so deeply that it drives you into yourself, where the muck and mire of Satan's lies destroys your ability to live. My college basketball experience unleashed the shame, and I had no idea what was happening to me.

During high school, our four year combined record was 85-7, with a fifty-two-game winning streak as part of the total. We were so successful that winning was a way of life and bolstered my self-worth without any effort. I was somebody, and throughout high school personal success in basketball camouflaged the damaging consequences of abuse.

The high school years are the most important time for development of self-esteem and image, and they mean the world to developing adolescents. I was living in two different worlds simultaneously, and learned to adapt my behavior to reflect so-called "normal" development. In fact, at the time, I perceived myself as comparable with my peers. All the winning protected me from the personal destruction that losing would have triggered. Looking back, I was blessed to be in that place and time in my life. I realize now that I was spared deep pain and suffering to my soul. I was living what I perceived to be a normal adolescent existence.

I was fortunate as a freshman in college to work my way into the starting lineup halfway through the season. I was ecstatic about the chance to play each game, and was a started with ten games left in the season. But the team struggled. We won only nine games. The following year as a young squad we only could muster nine wins again. I became cynical about the team, the college, and life in general. I loved playing basketball. And I believed that there was nothing I couldn't do on the court to prevent us from losing. What I had not learned was that team play and circumstances always trumps individual ability.

In high school I was blessed to be with great players. My coach was effective in preparing us, and we happened to be in a situation where the opposition was weak. In college, we were overmatched physically in most of our contests. My college coaches were outstanding men and tacticians. Coach Lee Pfund had been coaching at Wheaton for over thirty years and led Wheaton to its only NCAA national championship. Dick Helm took over my sophomore year at Wheaton and was an outstanding tactician. Coach Helm went on to coach in the NBA for eighteen years. My immaturity measured everything by winning, and since we lost consistently it had to be everyone else's fault, including my coaches.

In my mind losing equaled failure, and since I had not experienced that I proceeded to place the blame on everyone and everything.. I looked forward to the last two seasons with absolute determination to prove that I could do anything possible to make us successful.

Away from the court, college life had its crazy moments, and they were enough to take my mind off the court and ease the times of anger and discouragement. My roommate and the guys I hung around with were able to bring out the happy side in me, and that spring we ventured into a few college pranks that bring a smile and laugh to this day.

As physical education majors we all attended summer camp together as part of our education program. It meant eight weeks away from Jill in the woods of northern Wisconsin. However, the distance assured no chance of meeting with Uncle that summer. While I deeply missed Jill that summer, it was one of the best and worst experiences of my life.

The summer of 1974, after my freshman year at Wheaton, Jill and I were at the lake and she did it. She looked me in the eyes and said, "There's a way we can do it."

"Do what?" I asked.

"We can get married."

"You're crazy," I answered. "We have no money, no jobs, no place to live, and I'm still in school. It will never work."

My usual negative attitude of doom and gloom masked the fact that on the inside I was dancing with joy. She looked me in the eyes, and with that captivating smile she said, "Bill, will you marry me?" She took my line and she took my heart. Years later the realization of what that moment meant would chase me to my knees. Marriage is about love, unconditional love. It's not about escaping, secrets, and manipulating. For me it was a chance at freedom. What a terrible way to begin a marriage. I could stop the abuse and Uncle had promised me he would never touch me again. All would be well. I would be normal. We could move on. She will never have to know. I can have sex the way God intended, and we will live happily ever after. We talked about a date.

Needless to say, our parents were a bit hesitant about the idea. After all, we had no jobs, no money, and no place to live. We were nineteen and twenty years old. Our response to their concerns was, "We're going to get married sooner or later, so why wait?" Unofficially, plans began and we intended to announce in early October.

On September 1st my mother called me and said, all excited, "You're not going to believe this. Uncle Francis has booked a one-week vacation for you and him in Hawaii the week before you start school."

There was a long pause. "Mom," I responded, "I don't want to go."

"Are you crazy?" she said. "This is the trip of a lifetime. You have to go! And he's already bought the tickets." The door of freedom was just starting to open when it was slammed in my face. Satan found one more way to twist into my life. He was not going to go down without a fight.

We flew to Hawaii for a week stay, visiting three different islands. He made sure that this week would satisfy him. He had never demonstrated anger toward me during the eight years. Two nights before we flew home I stayed out late on the beach with some friends I made while trying to avoid contact back in the room. When I returned there were serious threats and physical and sexual contact that reached a dangerous level. I was scared for the first time. I was even more angry than scared, and I made up my mind he would not enjoy himself. I remember crying out to God to remove me from the moment. I am not sure exactly what an out-of-body experience is like. What happened that night must be close. He never touched me again.

Chapter 11

Marriage: The Great Escape

August 30, 1975. After all the planning and preparation, Jill and I exchanged vows and promised to stay
together forever. It was the traditional wedding with all the
bells and whistles. The day was filled with joy, and in that
moment we saw life ahead of us with challenges, expectations, and excitement. We found a place to live, had very
little money, no jobs; it didn't matter, we would live on love.
For me, our wedding night meant the end of evil. The abuse
I had experienced for seven years was over. I would share
love and joy and intimacy with Jill like it was supposed to
be. We headed to the Caribbean the day after the wedding
for a week of bliss. Two days into the honeymoon, one of the
coping behaviors I used to protect myself surfaced.

Someone forgot to tell me that living together twenty
four hours a day means at some point there has to be some
communication. I was always determined to avoid failure at
all costs. Failure can come in many ways, one of which is
fear of communicating lest you be perceived as an idiot. I
was afraid to ask the cab driver if we could get out early near
our hotel. Instead we drove four miles out of the way into
town. It meant we had to walk back to the hotel. Bewildered,
Jill asked me what the heck I was doing. "Why didn't you

just say something?" she pleaded. I couldn't respond that I was afraid, that I didn't want to impose on the cab driver, so I sheepishly said, "I don't know."

We walked back to the hotel in the afternoon Caribbean sun, without talking. Here we were, just a few days into our marriage, and Jill saw that all her work at getting me to communicate was going to be a bigger challenge than she realized. That night, I apologized. She shook her head and said, "Just talk."

The first two years of our marriage I was a full-time student. Jill graduated from nursing school the spring before we married and worked as a Registered Nurse. We had a little apartment near school and learned the ins and outs of living together. There were the usual newlywed disagreements that we smoothed over quickly. For the most part those years set a foundation for us as a couple. We were active in our church and found time to relax and enjoy each other's company.

On the basketball court I was determined the last two years to turn our team into a winner. There was a coaching change, and our team was gaining experience, which meant anticipation of a better year. Instead the year was a miserable failure from a winning perspective. I played with reckless abandon and believed I could win every game by myself. It produced anger that was toxic. People around me would say, "Bill is so competitive, he hates to lose." Unfortunately, what others perceived as a drive to win was mostly anger protecting my soul from the fear of failure. Everything was about me. If we lost, I was the reason we were losing. It spilled over into everything. My class work, fixing a leaky faucet at home, playing a simple board game—all were subject to anger and anxiety if there was the slightest error. Marriage erased the opportunity for any future abuse. However, the consequences of the years of abuse began to eat away at my soul like a slow-growing cancer. The last two years of college were a roller coaster of emotions between the game

I believed was the measure of my worth and a marriage that was stumbling through infancy.

The final year in basketball saw the team finish with a respectable 15-10 record. A two-point loss to Illinois Wesleyan University and Jack Sikma kept us out of post-season play. I was able to collect a number of personal accolades for my accomplishments, all of which came with a price. I sacrificed the camaraderie and a close relationship with my teammates for my own personal triumph. I don't believe it was selfish intent, in fact that is so far from the real me, yet I was guilty of allowing the lies of my failed self-worth to cloud what could have been a true team experience. While the awards and recognition provided some measure of achievement on the outside, on the inside, the platitudes were shallow.

There were no problems with physical contact, at least on the surface. If, however, intimacy is the connection of two people that love each other unconditionally and share that love through a physical union as God designed as intimacy, well, we didn't have that. We had sex. That's what married couples do. It was satisfying and I believed it demonstrated that I really cared for her. I didn't realize at the time that I had no idea what intimacy really was. For that matter, what newlyweds do have a grasp of true intimacy? Where do you learn about intimacy other than journeying together through the experience and learning as you grow? I never allowed growth to happen. There was no emotional connection. There was no desire for closeness. I was a machine. I had no idea that my inability to connect on an emotional and spiritual level with Jill was important. My experience with intimacy was taught to me by an evil man with evil intentions. There was never an emotional or spiritual component to the abuse. I behaved the way I had been taught. Certainly it was an unacceptable reason for failing to connect with Jill, and it was definitely not an acceptable excuse for failing to pursue a healthy marital intimacy. While ignorance is inexcusable as well, the damage done by the abuse was deeper than I ever understood. As we walked the early path of marriage, I was not building a bond that would bring joy, trust, and connection; I was just performing.

Despite the baggage I brought into our marriage, all in all, the first two years together were good times. We lived on a shoestring budget and learned to manage. We learned how important it was to make time for each other. We were moving in a positive, healthy direction.

Chapter 12

Living the American Dream

I graduated from Wheaton in June of 1977 and accepted a teaching position in Rockford, Illinois. Jill became pregnant in the fall of '76. Our first child was due in August, and as it would happen she was born the day I began my teaching/coaching career. Just five pounds six ounces, we welcomed our beautiful little girl Jaimee home.

The first year in teaching is all about keeping your head above water as you try to stay just ahead of your students. With a brand new baby at home, it was difficult to focus on the job because I was so eager not to miss a moment with Jaimee. Jill and I learned on the fly the joys and pains of parenting. We were grateful for the nurturing of our own parents during those early sleepless nights. Despite the challenge of a new marriage, career, and daughter, the first two years were packed with incredible memories. I was a daddy, and nothing in the world meant more to me than being with her every minute.

Like all babies, Jaimee changed very quickly. I remember one story in particular when Jaimee and I were driving home from church one Sunday morning. Jaimee was a precocious, joyful child. She was in the front seat (seat belts and car seats hadn't crossed anyone's mind yet), and we were discussing what she learned in Sunday school that morning. She gave me a quizzical look and asked, "Daddy, does Jesus live up in the sky?"

"Well, yes I believe He does" I replied.

She paused for a moment then turned and asked, "Daddy, does Jesus live in my heart?"

I smiled at her and said, "If you want him to he surely will."

She thought for a moment and then turned to me with a big smile on her face and said, "Man, is he tricky".

The new school was one of the pioneers in the Christian education movement. It began with a kindergarten through third grade program and added a grade level or two each year. When I arrived they had progressed through the 11th grade. The high school was small and didn't have a full-time physical education teacher. When I was hired, I asked the Principal if I could start an athletic program in the high school. His response was, "Sure you can start whatever you want. You don't have any money, but have a great time." I could not believe my good fortune. I was a first-year graduate with the responsibility of developing a high school athletic program.

Imagine that—me, a coach. It was the natural course of events. I was a physical education major, athletics was my expertise, and now I could give back to young athletes all that I had learned as a player. Never mind the huge impact winning and losing had on developing my self-esteem in high school and college. Never mind that the pitfalls of losing in the coaching arena may highlight the lack of worth I still carried inside from the abuse. This was the chance to redeem myself and secure the illusive dream of a championship. Call it naivety, call it youthful arrogance, it didn't matter. Just get out of my way because I am going to make this happen. I will prove to the world that I am the best coach out there.

Jill and I were developing the American dream in the tradition of Cleaverville. The cynicism and disdain I had developed toward the church late in high school and college softened following our marriage and my last two years in college. Maintaining a good image was important to us. We wanted to portray to everyone a functioning marriage, successful employment, faithful church membership, and responsible loving parenting. Carrying on the tradition of our families and being perceived in a positive light was very important to Jill and me.

In 1979 our son, Jeffrey, was born. I had a son; life as a parent was now complete. He and I would play baseball, basketball, and football, and we would start as soon as he could stand up. He would be my all-American boy.

Jeffrey was very active as a toddler. One day he was in his walker and decided to go down the basement stairs by himself. Head first he tumbled down to the basement floor without suffering a bump.

Life was unfolding as expected. However, there was something that was traveling along with me that went unnoticed. I had learned by now all the coping mechanisms needed to cover and camouflage the damage the abuse had done without knowing that's what I was doing. I immersed myself in my work. I justified it as the development of a new athletic program at school, and with the limited resources it meant either I had to do all the work, or it wouldn't get done. The third year on the job, I was teaching seven classes a day and coaching two levels of three different sports. It just had to be done, I reasoned. If we were going to compete with the local public schools I had to spend the time in the trenches. What I missed was what that meant at home. Fourteen to sixteen hour days for the whole school year meant leaving the young family on the back burner.

Shame from abuse developed in me an unending fear of failure. As a result, I did anything I could to avoid being perceived as a loser. In the athletic arena that is easy to understand. As a coach I challenged the players every day to be the best they could be. In truth, I drove them to win because I needed them to win to demonstrate that I was valuable. If we lost, it wasn't me, it was the players. And yet I always took the losses harder. Away from the job, though, I always perceived little mistakes as major failures of me as a man. It could be the littlest thing, like forgetting to pick up a gallon of milk on my way home from work that Jill had specifically asked me to remember. I would agonize for hours about the mistake. If I couldn't get the grass to turn green in the yard each summer I would spend days in a terrible mood believing I as a person was a total failure. No matter what the activity, fear of making a mistake oftentimes would paralyze me. What will people think? They will see me as a failure. I will never measure up to everyone's expectations. I must do whatever I can to avoid that. In the early years it wasn't a constant issue. Every once in a while if things didn't go just right these thoughts emerged from seemingly nowhere. I always dismissed them as my competitive nature, and yet inside I believed they were true.

Silence and secrets were the coping mechanisms I used to cover my fear of failure. Being the competitive athlete I am, I embraced coaching as the lifeline to demonstrate to everyone that I was valuable. When everyone noticed how successful I was as a coach, they would then value me as a person.

It never dawned on me that my motives were misdirected. I was just adjusting to life. Unfortunately, the very nature of competitive athletics involves losing as much as it does winning. It means there is a constant striving to win in order to justify yourself as worthy. The definition of insanity is not far from this. I needed to prove my worth, but in proving it I would have to win in a nearly impossible arena. I embraced the pursuit, not realizing I was just enabling the wounds to fester.

Meanwhile at home, the duties of diapers and feedings and discipline required constant attention. My upbringing in both family and church prepared me for the basics of parenting, and I was able to manage quite well. Discipline was consistent, firm, and fair. Jill and I partnered in the responsibilities, and we modeled strong effective parenting to the community.

After just five short years and a very successful development of the athletic program, I received a call to return to Wheaton College to work as an assistant coach and pursue a graduate degree. I was just twenty-seven years old, with an opportunity to move up the coaching ladder quickly. As a bonus we were moving back home near family and friends. It was a wonderful opportunity, and Jill and I agreed it was in our young family's best interest.

Life was progressing just as we anticipated. A new job at a prestigious college granted me a respected place in the community. Faithful church attendance and well-behaved children developed a positive perception of a young, adjusted, loving family. What the outside didn't see nor did I recognize during those first five years was the lack of depth in my relationship with Jill. I was a robot, fulfilling all the expectations of a successful husband and parent yet failing to grow and nurture my wife. The outside never saw the anger that bubbled just below the surface when the slightest thing went wrong. I had a disabling fear about trying anything new outside my safe arena. I avoided any opportunity to make new acquaintances. Taking the time to get to know someone and then determine if they could be trusted was too much work, and too dangerous. As long as I could develop the perception that we were an all-American family without having to relate or talk to anyone, that would be just fine.

I never attempted to validate my wife for her role, her courage, her support, or her ability to deflect my weaknesses. While I endeavored to develop an ultra positive perception to the public, I stifled our relationship at home with silence, fear, and manipulation of feelings. Rather than open up to Jill about work, or discouragements, or even joys, I would hold it all inside. It wasn't purposeful. I wasn't trying to hurt her. I always felt awful after a disagreement or argument at the way I treated her. Rather than admit error, I would crawl in a hole and shut her out. I could not be wrong at any cost. Sometimes it took days, and it was usually Jill who made the first move at either reconciliation or just communication.

I was too emotionally disabled to know the right methods of behavior. I had learned early in our relationship that Jill would do all the work whenever difficult situations arose. She would handle difficult phone calls, difficult confrontations, our finances, and anything that required a hard decision. If it alleviated tension, confrontation, or just sheer silence, Jill did all the work of mending.

I was just fine with the physical part of our marriage. I understood passion. The chance of us growing together in intimacy was eroding right from the early years. I didn't know there was a difference between physical passion and genuine unconditional intimacy that flowed from the heart. Jill tolerated and patiently worked at fixing my odd behavior.

Chapter 13

The Darkness behind the Silence

Within one year of returning to Wheaton I found myself as the team's head coach. Head coach at twenty-eight—quite an accomplishment on the surface. Truth be known, it was through a series of uncontrollable circumstances that it came to be. Regardless, I was in the position and determined to make the most of it. I relished the idea that I was perceived as a successful young coach in a highly competitive conference. I continued to develop the expected perception of hard-working and committed coach, loving and caring husband and father, and dedicated member of church and community. Our second daughter, Julee, was born in 1984, and we continued pursuing the perception of a model family. It was during these years that Jill began to travel and sing with the girls. Jaimee started at age five and Julee at 3 three. Churches and community groups from all over the Chicago area invited the trio for banquets and special events. At one point we developed a family program with music and speaking, and my son, Jeff, and I joined the program. We were a strong, positive, image of the perfect evangelical family.

Unfortunately, when the consequences of abuse are not confronted, they slowly erode the soul like a growing cancer. My children were now old enough to observe my erratic behavior. I never missed one of their school or special events. I had wonderful moments coaching little league soccer, basketball, and baseball, but they cowered when I would rage about the littlest things. They distanced themselves when I reverted to the world of silence. They just knew during those moments not to bother dad.

The basketball team struggled to maintain a winning record, and losing games at the college began to take a toll on my heart and attitude. I withdrew further and further into myself. My erratic behavior, silence, and fear of failure began to take a toll on Jill. She had been the rock in our relationship, the one that held it together. She retreated from me for the first time, and I didn't know what to do. Without realizing it, she was calling me out. This had never happened before. I was always able to bring her back with some lame apology, crocodile tears, or repentant behavior. It had gone on too long, and she was tired of always being the one to smooth things over, to lead at home, and to reach out to new people. It was time to give me some of my own medicine.

I was at a loss. I never thought that the abuse attributed to my discontent. We crossed the Eleven-year mark in our marriage. I settled into a pattern of behavior that was safe for me. I never considered her feelings or the feelings of the children. It was all about protecting myself when life grew difficult. Jill had to carry all the emotions for the family, because when circumstances deteriorated, I just withdrew to the safe place of silence.

It never dawned on me that at the core, the root of this was the shield I raised so long ago. I just kept returning to what worked in the past. Instead of seeking help, or letting down my guard, or reaching out to the one who saved me, I went even deeper into the darkness, distancing Jill even further from my heart. I couldn't believe she wouldn't come running to my aid and smooth everything over. Instead, she moved away emotionally and physically, and although we were in the same house, we grew apart. This was unacceptable. I did everything she asked of me. I provided home and food. I showed how affectionate I was physically. I cared and managed the children without exception. All she had to do was appreciate all I did. Instead, she decided that communicating with a mute had gone far enough.

In the midst of all this growing tension she became physically ill. For two years the complications caused by a relatively new condition called Chronic Fatigue Syndrome relegated her to bed, sometimes 18-20 hours a day for weeks at a time. I was certainly capable of managing the house and the children, and I took over all the daily needs. Jill needed more. She needed me. By now I was so ensnared in self-protection that I had no idea what to do. My inconsiderate, insensitive behavior was destroying our marriage. Jill was tired of trying to change me.

Despair is the last stage before death. I found ways to stay away from church. I distanced myself from family, not physically, but emotionally I became a zombie. I had never allowed anyone to get close to me, so that was not an issue for me. The frustration and powerlessness I felt began to bring about a darkness I can hardly describe. I would sink into deep times of darkness as if a cloud would descend on me and there was nothing I could do to break out of it. The thought that at the core was the abuse of the past never crossed my mind. I believed it was my failure as a coach, my failure as a husband. I was the problem; no one could fix this; I was a loser and a failure.

I imagine someone reading this may think, "my goodness, Bill, it happened seventeen years earlier. Get over it. Move on. Everyone deals with problems and has bad things that happened to them in the past." The faith community taught me that it was my responsibility to get closer to God, work harder on my faith, and get into the Word more. You just aren't trusting God enough. I hated Sundays. I grew up in the church. I know and understand the truth. I will never leave my Lord who has prepared the way for me, but I wrestled with doubt like Jacob and the angel since the moment the abuse began. Often I have asked Jesus, "Why did you allow this to happen? How could you stand by and just let him do that to me? Why didn't you punish him?"

On Sundays I would hear the truth about how our sin nature lends itself to failure. Sundays just affirmed for me what I already knew. I am a guilty, shameful, lying, deceitful failure. Church was just another place away from home where I put on the mask and played the part, while inside the turmoil raged on. How could God love me?

Chapter 14

Failure Exposed

Time truly does move by quickly, and I had just completed my ninth year at Wheaton when the athletic director called me into his office. It was time for the yearly evaluation, and I expected the same routine. Instead, what I heard on the outside was "we are moving in a new direction." What I heard on the inside was *You are a failure. Who do you think you are? You can't coach. You can't lead young men. You are a loser, you have always been a loser, and you will always be a loser. Now what are you going to do, phony? This time you can't hide it. Everyone will see what you know inside. Your wife is sick, you have no job, and you are a failure. Now what?*

My brother-in-law graciously provided me with a job for the next year and a half while I tried to regroup. The pain and the everyday thoughts of failure continued to tear at my soul. Life seemed futile. I couldn't expose my feelings now and affirm my incompetence. I couldn't expose anything about my past and hurt my parents and extended family. I was still trapped after all those years, and I still kept it all inside.

The children always adjusted to me, my moods, and whatever was happening, and I managed to maintain an image and standing in the community that covered the despair. I was learning a new profession that was barely providing for our needs, and after nine months on the job, I remember sitting at the train station in Wheaton for what seemed like hours trying to gather up the courage to step out on to the tracks and end it all. No one knew the depth of the pain, or the level of darkness in my soul. I still did not connect the abuse of my past to what I was experiencing. I had kept it quiet all those years, and now my life was unraveling. I didn't understand why I was standing on the tracks, other than the fact that I felt there was no hope. I had failed. Standing there crying, not understanding what the abuse now nearly twenty years before had done to my soul, I wasn't coward enough to get in front of the train, so I returned home, bringing the silence and confusion with me.

Covering the past requires a lot of energy. I had to be on my toes all the time to keep the truth veiled. I settled into the routine and accepted the truth that this was to be my lot. Keep food on the table for my children, provide all the necessities for my wife, and project to my family and community that I was strong and able to come back from adversity. Just suck it up and quit feeling sorry for myself and get on with life. I had done it before, I could do it again.

Chapter 15

Just When I Needed It Most

After a year as an apprentice carpenter, I was approached about a position in a local Christian High School. While the year working in the trades helped us survive financially, it really wasn't what I felt was my calling. I met with the administrator from the school, and without even hearing a salary offer, I took the position.

This was a new beginning, a new lease, a chance to start over and prove to everyone I was still worth something. I was hired for the position of principal. Impressive, considering I had no experience in administration. I was a physical education major, for heaven's sake. I had no direct experience in this role. It didn't matter; as long as they were willing to hire me I was thrilled to have a position back in education. Naturally, there was a little apprehension, but it was completely overshadowed by my desire to succeed.

The children were wonderful during my year in transition. In particular our oldest daughter, Jaimee, was distinguishing herself as an excellent performer, both in music and drama. Jaimee started singing with Jill at the age of five doing banquets and church outings. She joined a local children's chorus and auditioned and secured a position in the prestigious Lyric Opera in Chicago.

Often during the transition year the struggle to recover a sense of value permeated my behavior. That spring, Jaimee developed a slide show with her own vocal backup and presented it at the annual junior high school variety show. She did a tribute to all the men and women that were serving in Desert Storm in Kuwait. I was so proud of her. It was a shining moment that spring. Jaimee went on to have the leading role in three productions in high school. I only wish now that at the time I had demonstrated to her how very proud I was of all of her accomplishments and for the respite from the despair she provided for me that year.

Jill was growing stronger and decided that spring to take a job part time helping a woman who cared for disabled children. It meant a little income, a chance for her to slowly assimilate back to the workforce, and it lifted her spirits to be out of the house. The home had anywhere from five to nine children at a time with all sorts of physical needs. It was a staging place until permanent placements could be found for the children.

After a week or two it became very clear that there were too many children at the home, and that it was difficult to provide the care they all needed. Jill volunteered to bring one of the children home on the weekend to ease the load. Her name was Jaime. She was six months old at the time, and she had multiple disabilities including cerebral palsy in all four limbs. She was unable to take a bottle, and had a significant brain injury that provided a prognosis that was not promising. Jill consulted with me and the children about bringing Jaime home for the weekend. We were all in agreement, and thought that a weekend or two would be a good experience for all of us. We never dreamed at the time what this would mean to our family.

Jaime was adorable. She had to be fed with a tube through her nose, and it was uncomfortable for the kids and me to watch when Jill would pull the tube out. Jaime didn't seem to mind. For the kids and I it was an immediate adjustment.

The weekend was a big hit, and the children really enjoyed her visit. She seemed much like any child at this age. Her disabilities were not very pronounced. We were all in agreement that should the need arise again, we would love to have Jaime come back for a weekend.

Just two weeks later, the caregiver informed us that Jaime would have to return to the care center because she could not keep her lawfully. Jill approached us with this idea. "Why don't we take Jaime on a temporary basis until they can find a permanent home? Putting her in an institution will not provide the best care." We all agreed. That weekend Jaime came to live with us. Problem number one, we already had a daughter named Jaimee. We quickly took turns on names, and since it had to start with the letter "J," mom suggested Joree. It stuck.

The original plan for six weeks rapidly came and went. Joree was fitting into a routine. Jill taught her how to take a bottle and began to teach her to eat. Losing the feeding tube was a great day. We bought new car seats, new bike seats, and toddler clothes. Six months went by very quickly, and she was already a part of the family.

There was an ongoing tussle with Children and Family Services about permanent placement or adoption. As she grew, her physical issues began to indicate that things were going to be very complicated as she aged. But there was something about her smile, something about her personality that charmed everyone, and the thought of her leaving became a sticking point. We received a phone call from DCFS one day informing us they were coming to get Joree because we had not made a commitment to permanent placement and adoption. My kids circled the wagons. They placed chairs, toys, and themselves behind the front door. "They'll have to go through us to get her, Dad," they declared with authority.

DCFS never did show up, although they threatened this action a couple more times. Each time, the realization that Joree was part of our family became clearer. I never imagined at the time the impact this little girl would have on my healing journey.

Chapter 16

The Darkness Returns

Learning and adjusting to a new position is always a challenge. I learned quickly the demands the role required, and was able to incorporate much of my coaching experience into the new job. Fortunately, I was working with an incredible group of people. They were supportive, encouraging, and committed to their task. Unfortunately, I was able to maintain a strong positive image that they followed and respected faithfully. I was able to mask the challenges I continued to battle inside.

Leaving Wheaton College had a deeper impact than I first realized. The loss of the coaching position fed my failure complex as I lived over and over the unfairness I perceived in the firing. It didn't matter that there were circumstances outside my control. The reality for me was that I had failed. It was hard to live in the neighborhood and have to meet neighbors and friends. The question always arose, "How are things at the College?" It fed the lies in my head that I was worthless. Surely everyone perceived me as a loser. I was worthless, and everyone viewed me as a loser. On the other hand, the perceived failures were very humbling, and I learned patience and compassion throughout the experience that I wouldn't realize until years later. The refining process is slow and painful. When I was in the middle of the turmoil, it was hard to recognize that any good was happening. I learned slowly the value of listening to others' viewpoint first. I also learned slowly that gaining people's admiration or affirmation did not have to be my goal. I had the false illusion that it was my responsibility to impress a person rather than value them and their ideas.

The principal position was very challenging, and I worked hard to learn as quickly as possible. It wasn't long before I had a good sense for the routine. The position required a lot of public relations. I had to develop and refine my public persona. I was able in this new environment to be very convincing as a leader and mentor to teachers. They were supportive, loyal, and gracious in following my lead. However, it became clear that I could no longer use the coping mechanisms I had used for so many years. Silence was not an option, and so while at school I played the confident, enthusiastic, together leader. At home the darkness that lingered just under the surface kept intruding. It became more difficult to manage the duplicity that I was living. The dark cloud swirled frequently, and often I welcomed it and didn't even try to break free. It was exhausting to maintain the image at school and return home to do battle with the darkness in my secret world. The children were older now, and able to see the changes. They learned their own behaviors to deal with my moods. Jill withdrew again. She was not going to go through this anymore. I couldn't blame her; I was awful to her. I thought it was acceptable behavior. Rather than have verbal arguments and confrontation, it was easier to just not talk about it and retreat to the basement, or television.

I had no desire to change because I didn't see myself as the problem. Tension around the house continued to grow so bad that I began to search for answers. Occasionally Jill would say to me with a smile, "I know everything there is to know about you." On cue I always responded, "You can never be sure you know everything there is to know about someone." It infuriated her. So many times I wanted to share with her about the past. I wanted to tell her I hadn't always been this way, but . . . but the weight of the shame always kept it inside; I just couldn't get it out.

Nineteen ninety-four was my third year at Aurora Christian School. In October I received a phone call with disturbing news. My mom was on the other end of the phone, and with a shaky voice she said, "Bill, we are at the hospital. Dad has had a stroke or something. We aren't sure yet, but it doesn't look good."

I jumped in the car and made the hour drive to meet with dad and the doctors. They gathered us all together and announced that Dad had a brain tumor that would have to be removed as soon as possible. When the doctors left and we all had a moment to process the news, Dad looked at me quietly and said, "Son, we will just have to trust God for the best."

My dad was my hero. From my earliest remembrances, I knew him as a gentle, happy man who embodied what he believed. He never missed a day of work in his life; he never said anything unkind about anyone at any time. He modeled for me a committed, caring husband and father his whole life, and so this moment seemed so unfair. Why, Lord? Why dad? He has been so faithful. He is just sixty-eight years old. I pleaded with God to allow him just a little more time.

Dad was my biggest fan. He instilled a love for athletics in me at the age of six. He coached my little league teams, enrolled me in basketball in fourth grade, and as I progressed through the years never once missed a game I played.

Dad was the oldest of eleven children. His family lived in a small two-bedroom apartment on the north side of Chicago in the thirties. He finished high school after returning from the war, met my mom, married, and went to work earning a living and raising a young family. He was the happiest man on earth and brought a smile to everyone he met. He loved working as a salesman because it meant he could interact with people all day. There was never a concern about bringing in big numbers because I believe he enjoyed the interaction more than the business side. Too often, Dad was just too nice, an attribute I treasure about him to this day.

The doctors removed dad's tumor in October. The first two months following surgery went very well. We played golf a couple of times and kept praying for healing. Unfortunately, the tumor returned, and despite seven weeks of radiation treatment the doctors discussed a second surgery. The radiation continued to weaken his body, and by May he was failing quickly. We shared Father's day together reminiscing about so many memories. Two weeks later we were together in his home when the Lord called him home. There was never a doubt in my mind of his devotion to me. He never knew about the abuse I suffered. Looking back, I regret in a way that he didn't know. He would have been very angry and may have sought revenge. I know for sure he would have come alongside me and walked through the pain of healing. He was a gentle man with a huge heart. I understand now that much of his modeling and commitment are part of me and have been with me through my journey. Hundreds of people, many I did not know personally, visited with us and attended Dad's funeral. They all spoke of his kindness, his compassion, and his joy. I miss him a lot.

A year after Dad died, in the midst of growing inner turmoil, we made the decision to bring Joree into our family permanently. We pursued all the paperwork, and on April 22, 1996, Joree officially became our daughter. Jill and I and the children had discussed all the implications at length. There was no confusion about what it would mean to care for her. None of that swayed us from our choice. We all believe God placed her in our home and she placed herself in our hearts forever.

Shortly after the adoption an opportunity to return to the school where I began teaching presented itself, and I agreed to go. I took over as the middle school principal and was given the high school boys' basketball head coaching position. My son, Jeff, was going into his junior year, and I would be able to coach his team. Fifteen years had gone by since we left Rockford for Wheaton, and yet there was a sense of coming home.

The school had grown to over 1000 students, and the basketball team had great potential for the years ahead. With Dad gone it allowed us the chance to move near my mother and sister. Our daughter Jaimee was attending Moody Bible Institute, and our second daughter Julee was a sixth grader. While it was a distance from our home, there was a marvelous school for children with disabilities, so we felt very satisfied that Joree's special needs would be met. All in all, we all felt good about making the move.

While things on the surface appeared to be together and moving forward, on the inside, I had reached a breaking point. May 26, 1996, I asked Jill to meet me for lunch. I told her I had something very important to tell her. She kept asking on the way to the restaurant what it was all about. We never talked anywhere, so why would we be going out to talk? She was suspicious.

After several uncomfortable moments mustering up all the strength I had, I blurted out, "I was abused."

Startled, Jill responded, "What?"

I fumbled the words out again. "I was abused as a kid, sexually."

The emotion got the most of me, and tears welled up in my eyes. I did not cry in front of Jill very often. For the first time in twenty-one years the secret was out. She knew. It was as if the "weight of the world" had been lifted off my shoulders. She peppered me with questions. "Who did this? When? Why didn't you tell me?" I gave her enough information for her to begin to understand some of the whys of my behavior all these years.

That night we cried together. Holding each other felt different. I felt connected; I felt at peace. Long ago I believed getting married would eliminate the past. Marriage would free me from the abuse and I could move forward with life the way it was intended. Instead, the dark seed in my soul grew slowly and sinisterly into fear. The fear multiplied into mistrust. Finally, shielding the secret from the world, my soul sunk into despair. But this night, the veil was lifted. The secret was out. This time, I could put it all behind. The chains were off. Now I would be free. Now I could truly start living.

Chapter 17

Facing the Past

The new position in Rockford and the recently disclosed information made for an interesting summer. With four years of experience as a principal now under my belt, I felt comfortable about continuing in a similar role. Even better, I was back coaching. It was second nature to me, and the prospects for a successful program ignited a new enthusiasm and determination for the year ahead.

With the revelation of my past, somehow I assumed my behaviors and attitude toward life would demonstrate a growing improvement. Jill would view me with compassion. My odd and erratic behaviors would now be recognized, and if I used any of the long-practiced coping strategies, Jill would understand and cut me some slack. It wasn't my fault; I'm not responsible; I was abused; I am a victim. The pain of disclosing was out, and now I could rest easy, even if I behaved the same way.

Jill went right to work attempting to fix my past. She wrote a certified letter to my uncle. He returned the receipt. She informed him clearly that his secret was out and that the damage he had done was unthinkable. How could he live with himself, knowing of all the pain and suffering he had inflicted on me? Her determination to confront him directly with the truth may have contributed to Uncle's downfall. Two months later, he died. I didn't have the opportunity to see him again face-to-face once the secret was out. I had not progressed to a point where I desired to forgive him, and I chose to not attend the funeral.

Jill believed it was important to gather support around me, and that everyone would understand and come alongside me with words of encouragement and understanding. Sharing with the children would put them at ease and explain a lot of my curious behaviors. I was not ready for that yet. I wasn't ready for the whole world to know. Jill's determination to fix the past backfired when the people she told weren't ready to handle the information. She shared the story with my mother and grandmother. Grandma's response was surprising but not unexpected. It was her brother, after all, and she felt that disclosing family secrets this long after the fact would not benefit anyone. "Just leave the past in the past" she said, "There's no benefit in bringing all that up now."

Keeping the abuse secret was driven mostly by the fear of what others would think. I feared the looks. I feared they would treat me differently. Most of all, I wasn't over the shame. Once again I retreated into my safe world of solitude and silence. No way was that going to work this time. What happened next only reinforced for me why I had remained quiet for so long. Jill insisted we see a counselor, something I had absolutely refused in the past. I reluctantly agreed.

We were directed to a local Christian counselor, and for the second time I told my story. Trusting an unknown person with the deepest pain and personal heartache was a huge step forward. It took me the whole session to relive as much of the past as I could recall at the time. I remember leaving once again feeling free and peaceful. Letting it out unleashed a flood of emotions I had never experienced. There was joy, and a sense of euphoria I experienced after great moments in the classroom or on the basketball court. I was excited that the ever-present sense of fear was lifting a little.

The second session, the counselor decided that the severity of the abuse and the long amount of time that had transpired since left me susceptible to evil, dark forces. He turned off the lights in his office and quietly announced he would perform an exorcism on me to remove all the evil spirits. In just one hour he set me back two years. I heard the accusations in my soul again. *It's your fault all of this happened. You are the one that allowed this to go on. You could have changed this. You are so disgusting. You think this counselor can help you now? You will never be free from this. I told you it would be a mistake to let the secret out.*

I limped home. Meeting Jill at the door, I said, "That's why I never went to a counselor. That's why I will never go again. He just told me what I already know. I am the problem. I allowed my uncle to abuse me all those years. I am dirty and a failure. You can't fix this. Don't you dare try talking to me right now."

I retreated to the basement and stayed there all night. I was seething with anger. The next morning Jill asked what happened. In a hateful, anger-filled response I yelled, "I wish I had never told you what happened. Everything would have been fine. It was so much better when no one knew about this. I told you counselors are idiots!"

I poured out all the anger, guilt, and shame on Jill. It was all I knew, and while it was so wrong and so selfish, it was the way I protected my heart and feelings. I had to go back where it was safe for me. This was way too painful. I didn't want to relive this all over again. People were just going to have to accept me for me and get over it. I retreated to living where I felt the safest. I didn't talk about anything that had transpired the last year. It was back to status quo.

Chapter 18

Chasing the Dream

M y son's senior year the team finished 27-2. They set all kinds of records. It was a Hoosiers experience, with the extra bonus of coaching Jeff. He was a great team leader, and at times I put expectations on him that were unrealistic. He accepted his role and, more incredible, he tolerated his coach.

Watching Jeff perform was the highlight of my coaching career. The sense of pride seeing him excel filled the season with joy and excitement. The local news media was obsessed with the team's progress. Rockford is big enough to have its own television stations, yet removed enough from a large city that local news and sports dominate the coverage. Every Friday night we were covered with highlights and special spots on the team's progress. As the season unfolded the winning streak became a bigger story, and by mid-February there was talk of a successful state championship run. In Illinois, that is about as big as it gets in high school athletics. Making it to the "Sweet 16" is the dream of every player and coach from the time they began playing. In the eyes of the city and all of northern Illinois, we were pretty special. I embraced the attention with pride, and it served to ease the turmoil I had been experiencing. I was in a good place for three months.

The team rambled through the state playoffs, won the school's first conference championship, and advanced to the first round of the state sectionals. At 27-1 and ranked in the top ten in the state, things looked great for the team to make a run to the finals. Standing in the way was the only team we had lost to earlier in the year. Ironically, this game was played on the same neutral court as the first one in the fall. Entering the fourth quarter we had a six-point lead. Just eight minutes and we would go farther than any other team in school history. My twenty years of coaching experience were paying off. Then it happened: the coach out maneuvered me and took the lead with just two minutes left and we could not recover. We came up six points short.

Disappointment filled the locker room. It is hard to describe the depth of the pain you feel in those moments. After a year of dedication and sacrifice, the dream of being a champion is cut short in just a moment. Over the years, I observed that players hurt for a few hours and then they move on. This group was the same. They had an incredible year filled with lifelong memories and would be remembered as the best team ever.

The experience for me with Jeff was irreplaceable. Yet, as great as it was, when the dust settled, I once again second-guessed my every move. *We came up short, and it was my fault. I failed once again. I don't deserve to reach the top. God will never allow me to be a champion. It must be because I don't deserve it. I am so unworthy, God must be punishing me for all of my failures.* I knew theologically I was way off base, but doubt and fear of God, for an abuse survivor, often overshadow what we know to be the truth. *God wasn't there when I was abused; He must have been punishing me then, so why would things be any different now? You can spin it anyway you want and focus on all the positive aspects all you want, the fact is we didn't make it to the top and therefore I'm still a failure.* I returned to my quiet world, where I felt safe and comfortable. Living in the world of self-pity and silence was easier than making excuses for my failure. The world of honesty and communication were much too difficult. I just returned to the world I knew best.

Two years after I disclosed my awful past, things had not really changed. Thirty years of abuse and silence will not be healed in three days, three weeks, or three years. It is a permanent injury that has lifelong complications. Counseling didn't work, so I crawled back into my shell, conceded that there was no hope, and determined that I would just live the rest of life out the best I could.

A couple of weeks after the basketball season an opportunity presented itself at a large Christian school in Phoenix, Arizona. We considered for several years a move to a warm climate to assist Jill with all of her health issues. I interviewed for the position and had a real peace that it was the right move at the time. We packed up a truck and headed west. Forty-two years of good and bad memories would now be thousands of miles away. It was a chance to start over completely, a chance to travel down a new road, and a chance to reach for the hope of healing.

Chapter 19

Streams of Hope in the Desert

Northwest Christian School was very similar to Aurora Christian School, where I served as principal. They were looking for someone with experience in multiple areas. The first three years I taught eighth grade and assisted the head administrator with selected duties. When they asked if I was interested in coaching, I hesitated at first. They had a girls' position open. My daughter Julee was in eighth grade and a pretty accomplished player, so I decided to take the job. There was a lot less pressure from the outside; however, consistent with my history I made up for that with my own lofty expectations.

Circumstances developed where I was asked to take the high school principal position on an interim basis. I agreed, and for the next three years I served in that role. I continued to coach the high school girls' team and Julee for the rest of her high school career. Like coaching my son, Jeff, I cherish the memories.

Julee was around me in the basketball arena from birth. Jill's illness struck when Julee was just two years old, which meant that Julee spent a lot of time at the gym with me, where I could care for her. She learned the game through osmosis, is gifted with athletic talent, and has a competitive drive greater than most.

We did everything to prepare for a successful high school career. That preparation paid off in the end. Julee set a number of records that will last for a long time. Like with her brother, at times I placed the expectations pretty high for her, but she never complained and performed with heart and courage all the time.

Her senior year the team advanced to the Arizona state quarterfinals. The girls performed honorably and fell just five points short of advancing to the state finals. Julee's response was similar to Jeff's. She cried and shared her disappointment with her teammates, and then moved on. I decided that this was it. *A championship is not in the cards for me. You would think after all these years, sacrifice, and determination, God would work it out so I could win. But then again, I don't deserve it, so it's time to just give it up.*

Following the season I resigned from the girls' position only to have the athletic director offer me the boys' position. Without much hesitation I agreed. It didn't dawn on me that coaching for me was like a gambler living in Las Vegas. Someone who is addicted to a profession that assures failure should not be coaching, because the ultimate prize is nearly unattainable. You are always in a losing situation. But the allure of proving my worth always overshadowed the losses.

When we left Illinois there was an unspoken determination that this time it would truly be a new start. I would work hard at communicating my feelings to Jill and the children. I would welcome new people and opportunities into our life and not be afraid to fail. After all, I told my story to a counselor in Illinois. I would try to do the best I could from now on. But in just three short years the habits of the past returned. Jill had enough.

On a Friday afternoon she picked me up at school and informed me that we were on our way to Tucson to see a counselor. I lost it. Through the screaming and yelling, the protests of the worthlessness of counselors, she persisted. She laid out an ultimatum: if you don't do this, I am going to leave. The remainder of the two hour trip was in silence, with an occasional angry sigh or bang on the steering wheel. We arrived at the counselor's home, and before we went inside I said, "Fine, I will go through this for you, but I am telling you now, it won't make any difference. We can just pack up tomorrow and head home."

Jill failed to tell me that we were there until Sunday. When I heard that, I said in front of the counselor, "No way, I am going home tomorrow. I have told this story twice now, and each time I have been burned just like the abuse. What makes you think this time it will be any different? Go ahead and tell me something I don't already know."

That evening Jill shared about the last five years and my failure to make any improvement or change since I first disclosed the abuse. I filled in a few details, but was determined to just get through until the next day and then be out of there. Jill was there more for herself than she was for me. I had abused her all these years in ways she never deserved. She took it all until now. She had reached a breaking point, and this was the last stand.

The following day was spent telling the story again. As the day went by I unpacked more and more details, and at times the pain in my heart was so excruciating I felt physically ill. Memories reentered my mind that I had blocked out for years. I smelled the smells, I heard the sounds, I saw the images in my mind as if I was right there. I was exhausted. This was too much, and again the anger rushed to the surface. What good was this possibly doing? This is stupid. I had had enough and I shouted, "I am going home tonight!"

Patti looked directly in my eyes and spoke to me like no one ever had before. She said, "Fine, go home," with an intimidating tone. "Jill is staying the night. When we are finished, we will bring her home. You know, young man," she continued, "I really don't care what you do. If you are too big a coward to face this, then fine, go home and keep living the way you have all these years. But if you want to change and find out what you have been missing, you be here in the morning. And one more thing," she added. "I will leave this book with you. It doesn't matter to me if you read it; I'm not the one who needs help. At least do this for me—promise me you will read it someday."

With that she stood up and looked at me with an attitude of disgust and compassion, and said, "I am going to bed. If you are here tomorrow, great, if not, Jill and I will work together."

Patti had no idea how competitive I am. I took her admonition as a challenge. Out of pure stubbornness and anger I would prove her wrong. I stayed up the whole night and read the book from cover to cover. When she came in the next morning she found me on the couch. Somewhat sarcastically she said, "So, I see you are still here."

"I read the whole book" I responded.

"You did what?" she asked curiously. "I read the whole book, cover to cover. I never went to sleep."

"And what did you learn?" her voiced softer this time.

"I know I need help," I responded. "I hope there is hope for me. Can you help me get there?"

This time I truly surrendered. I let down my guard. I was ready to change. I felt really vulnerable. I read for the first time in Dan Allender's book *The Wounded Heart* that it wasn't my fault. I didn't choose to be abused. It profiled all the thoughts I wrestled with. It described my behaviors all these years. It convicted me of the truth that I had turned into an abuser myself. Jill had done nothing to deserve all the years of silence, of controlling, and of rejection. Yes, I was abused, but I did not have the right to take it out on my wife and children. For the first time in a long time I didn't see myself as a failure, as unworthy. I saw myself as wounded and in need of healing. I felt drained. The road ahead was daunting. I had lived this way for over thirty years, and this was not going to be easy. I had reached the bottom, and I felt slightly relieved to be looking up.

Patti and Jill spent the rest of the day holding me through the tears. Patti described strategies I was going to need to stop the lies that owned my heart and mind. I would have to work every day on this if I was going to reverse the habits so ingrained in my behavior.

Like many benchmark moments in our lives, I hoped this one would be a new beginning and I would not fall back into the old patterns too easily or quickly. I hoped I would have the strength to move on.

It has been several years since the meeting in Tucson. I know the strategies, I know the triggers. I know that it is my responsibility to work at this and not Jill's to enable or fix. I am making progress. But this is a devastating injury. There are so many twists and turns that involve family, friends, church, and employment on so many levels. Science is finding that there is actual damage done to the emotional centers in the brain. The damage leads to depression, fatigue, and anxiety. Millions succumb to addictive and dangerous behaviors, be it drugs, alcohol, or violence. Nearly one hundred percent of convicted criminals, both men and women, have a history of physical or sexual abuse.

So, is there any hope for long-term healing? There are medicines available that assist survivors in managing depression and despair. Professional counselors are equipped to provide therapy. Some churches reach out to the wounded with prayer and counseling support. But in the end, is there truly hope for healing and joy?

Hope is defined as a feeling that what is wanted will happen. My desire is to live without the pain, live without the memories, and live without the fear. I really want that to happen. Yet after all the years of hurt in my soul and the struggle to keep myself on an even keel, I don't believe I will ever be completely free in this life.

My daughter Joree's body is damaged beyond healing. She will never walk, never speak, and never eat on her own. Her twisted body suffers pain if she is adjusted with the slightest wrong movement. Twelve major surgeries in ten years have only done enough to slightly improve her quality of life. Every daily human function you and I take for granted is outside her control. And yet, in her infirmity every morning she greets me with a brilliant smile that brightens my morning. For Joree, and anyone who suffers from physical disabilities, hope for a feeling that what is wanted will happen is an exercise in futility. There is no hope for healing in this life for them. Likewise, for me and the millions that hope our souls will be healed in this life, despair disables that hope. Therapy, medication, prayer, and counseling improve the quality of life, but the hope for a feeling that what is wanted will happen, for us like for Joree, will never happen in this life.

If hope is not worth pursuing, why go on? If there is no hope of healing for Joree, why not just withhold the feeding tube and let her quietly drift into eternity? Where can we go? Who can answer our cries? It all seems so hopeless. It is, if we limit our view to just this life. There is no hope of healing for Joree in this life. There is no hope of healing for me in this life. But what about a next life?

The prevailing wisdom of the current culture is that God either does not exist or, if He does, He is a non factor. Therefore, any hope for utopia beyond this natural world is futile, non-rational thinking practiced by superstitious religious crazies completely out of touch with reality. And yet, I have a hunch that when the thought of a life beyond crosses everyone's mind, we all hope that there is truly something waiting—something that it is good—and that everyone will have a part of it.

In the Bible there is a verse that says, "Now faith is the assurance of things hoped for, the conviction of things not seen" (Hebrews 11:1). Dozens of people are highlighted throughout the Bible for their faith. They are not admired for their hope. Rewards are not distributed in this life because a person hoped for success. People are measured by the strength of their faith, and the benefits will be enjoyed in the life to come. The faithful set their eyes on the perfecter of their faith, Jesus Christ.

Jesus Christ. A name the prevailing culture of today and much of the world dismisses as insignificant. Yet He made a claim that if anyone chooses to follow Him and put their faith in the word He delivered and the work He performed, they would be granted perfection in the life to come. The hope is not in the feeling of something that is wanted; the hope rests in the assurance that the faith has merit. My faith then rests in what He said and what He did.

How does this impact Joree and me? Jesus Christ walked on this planet just like all the rest of us. He made and extraordinary claim that He was the Son of God. Making a claim is one thing, backing it up quite another. His words were enough and all that is needed to justify faith in Him, but there was much more. There were miracles of healing and miracles over nature. He walked the same roads we do. He experienced the daily struggles with physical and emotional needs we know. He experienced pain. He experienced broken friendships. People betrayed Him. At the height of His popularity, He was subjected to the cruelest form of abuse known to man. He suffered physical, verbal, and sexual abuse without just cause. All of the struggles Joree and I battle every day He experienced in His life. Who better to understand than someone who has been there? But the eternity thing, Bill, what does faith in Jesus have to do with eternity?

It is an undisputed truth that Jesus died. It is also an undisputed truth that He rose from the dead. Hundreds of eyewitnesses testified they saw Him. The man who claimed to be God in the flesh died and then returned from the dead with a healed, whole, perfect body. That's it. My faith rests in Jesus' word, "he who believes in Me will live even if he dies" (John 11:26). Life with a healed, perfect body just like the one He showed to the twelve.

I rest in my faith. The Bible says, "Without faith it is impossible to please [Jesus], for he who comes to God must believe that He is and that He is a rewarder of those who seek him" (Hebrews 11:6). I believe that same Jesus will give my precious Joree a new body when she dies. She will eat, sing, run, and dance. I believe He has a new body for me, too. No more wounded soul. Joy I hope for today will be mine because of my faith in His journey.

If this has been your journey, where does your hope rest? Someday you will wrestle in this healing journey with Jesus. You may not believe anything he did has any importance for you in your journey. You may be angry at him for not being there when your abuser stole your soul. Whatever your experience, one thing is certain, you cannot ignore Him. Like it or not, He is here with us today and He grieves with our pain, and hurts with failures. He promised us that if we don't let go, He will be there in the end. My faith is holding on to that hope.

Chapter 20

The Healing Journey

Healing from sexual abuse or any other kind of abuse is not an easy process. The injury goes so deep and involves so many different dynamics of life it becomes a long, complicated journey. Many times I hear well-meaning pastors or laypeople talk about forgiveness as if it is a quick fix-all. If you just muster up a little more faith, you can put this thing behind you. With all due respect, unless people have experienced the trauma, they really don't understand the layers and layers of shame that need to be systematically and carefully removed. It is so easy to re-victimize survivors with well-meaning simple solutions.

For me it was thirty years of silence; thirty years of developed coping behaviors. A couple of books, some counseling sessions, and lots of faith are the right start, but the pathway to healing is long, sporadic, and painful. The good news is that there are moments of joy and hope along the way that become more frequent, more welcome, and more encouraging. It becomes a battle I don't have to fight alone, and slowly I have found the happy little boy I knew long ago; the little boy whose innocence was stolen, the little boy who loved life like his father, the little boy who wanted so desperately to be accepted. I am getting closer each day.

Without question, the first step in the healing process is to tell the story. You have to go back to the moments in time and live and feel the pain. I recommend that you do this with a competent, trusting counselor that knows the nature of abuse and its consequences. Trying to go it alone is courageous, but the safety of a trusting professional will help get you off to the right start. Safety is an absolute must in the first stages of disclosure. You are sharing a part of you that is totally personal, and in most cases has never been shared. Be sure that the person you talk with is safe. It may need to be someone you do not know who will have an objective view of your story. In any case, be sure it is a trustworthy professional.

For some, writing the story the first time is just as therapeutic. Many counselors use this method to start and then encourage regular journaling through the healing process. The recall process will awaken forgotten memories and trigger feelings that have long been quieted. Writing is a very positive method in the healing process.

There are so many different stories of abuse; it is hard to lay out a specific model for healing. However, all abuse results in large amounts of shame, and until that, and the consequences it brings, are dealt with, it is hard to move forward. Dr. Steven Tracy, in his book *Mending the Soul: Understanding and Healing Abuse,* has a splendid model for healing, along with a clear and concise Biblical treatise on the healing path. He specifically outlines the pathway to healing by detailing the need to face the brokenness, rebuild intimacy with God, and progress to a level of forgiveness. Dr. Tracy's book is the best resource I know of for healing abuse from a Biblical perspective, and I highly recommend it in your journey.

Many times people comment, "just forgive and forget, move on, demonstrate a little more faith—that's what Jesus would do." There is no question that the ultimate goal is to reach a level where one reaches out in genuine forgiveness as a testimony of God's healing. Getting to that point will differ for all survivors. But to simplify the pathway or timeline is to seriously disrespect the level of damage abuse does. Forgiveness can be very complicated. It involves the victim and the abuser, both of whom will be in different stages of the journey. Survivors may take years to just be able to speak about the pain, and then more years to be able to rebuild themselves and their relationships with family, friends, and God.

There can be harmful models of forgiveness that can hurt as much as heal. The goal is to work toward a heart of forgiveness that will signify that you have experienced genuine healing and are moving away from the past. I wish I could tell you it is quick and easy. I have been traveling this healing road for nearly twelve years now. I am trying each day to change years of habits and behaviors. I have forgiven my uncle in my heart, even though I was never able to confront him in person. I am free from his hold. I am trying to rest in my Savior's arms, and I am making progress. There is hope; hold on with all you have.

One of the benefits of the healing journey is that once you have told your story and begun down the healing path, there is an intense desire to reach out to fellow wounded travelers. The initial joy and the steady promise of happiness motivate you to want to share it with the entire world. The good news that there is hope consumes your heart and mind. When you have done the hard work of healing there is unbridled enthusiasm to share the hope.

In the spring of 2006 I was about to complete my thirtieth year in Christian education. I was in line to take a high-level administrative position that would have secured my future into retirement years. I received a call about a ministry that was seeking an experienced administrator to assist with the development of the work. After listening to the job description and vision of the ministry, Jill and I believed that this was a clear calling from our Lord. It was the chance to develop a healing ministry for survivors of abuse, and the opportunity to tell my story at the same time. All the years would now have meaning and purpose. I accepted the position and began working in the summer of 2006.

It was so energizing to be on the frontline of a work that understood the nature and prevalence of abuse. I could not believe the magnitude of the problem and the need for intervention in so many places and lives. The ministry developed training programs for lay counselors in churches, and it developed the finest curriculum there is for helping survivors through the early healing process.

I discovered another issue that surrounds this ministry. This is Satan's turf. His hands are so intertwined with this issue and in the arena that trying to intrude and fight back is costly. The enemy has no intention of giving up the high ground, and I believe that with the advent of the Internet he has unleashed a weapon of mass destruction that is destroying this and future generations like none before.

The Internet has provided Satan with a tool to abuse children the same way men have been doing it forever, only now it is in the secrecy of a child's room. The consequences will be the same as if an actual person were perpetrating the crime. Guilt, shame, silence, powerlessness, will be multiplied by millions, and victims will stumble around totally clueless about why they are depressed. Satan will have stolen their innocence, stolen their God-given design, and stolen their ability for true happiness in this world.

Just twelve months after I began with the new ministry I was diagnosed with prostate cancer. Fifty-two years of age is relatively young to encounter any kind of cancer, but if it is diagnosed early prostate cancer is 95 percent curable. Regardless, the C word gets your attention very quickly. As an abuse survivor it also attacks the core issues of trust.

Where was God when I was being abused? Here I am now getting my life together, and what's the deal God, cancer? I am here and ready to serve you, to save others, to show how good and obedient I am. Why? Again the lies of Satan poured into my mind. This time, though, the healing I have done and the strategies to combat the enemy helped beat back the moments of despair.

I wrestled with insurance companies for three months about coverage for Proton Beam Therapy Treatment in California. I received the approval on October 15, 2006, and began treatment the 19th. Forty-five single daily treatments over a two-and-half-month schedule. It meant being alone in California away from Jill and family. It meant fighting Satan and my thoughts and the setback in my journey. It meant learning and hearing from God very clearly about His unending faithfulness and His incredible love for me. My faith was growing each day as I was able in solitude and silence to listen to His voice.

Just three weeks into the treatment, it became clear that the ministry I was with would no longer be able to employ me. "But, Lord, I gave up my career for this; I believed with all my heart this was your direction for us. How can this be? I have cancer and no job—what is happening?"

Again, lies from the pit of hell began to invade my fragile heart. "See, Bill, you are a loser, a failure; God doesn't care about this ministry of yours. Just give it up. Walk away; find another job, this one is going nowhere."

I completed the cancer treatments on December 26, 2008. I returned home physically weary from the daily radiation. My heart was heavy with the reality of no employment and the need for Jill to assume the role of provider. The discouragement moved me back to the dark side. Why, Lord? I have been making such good progress.

When I left my position at Northwest Christian School I agreed to continue on as basketball coach. I just couldn't walk away from the thing I love the most, and NCS was gracious to allow me to continue in that role. Just when I needed encouragement the most, I returned to the team after the New Year in 2008. It was an incredible group of young men, and the coaches had prepared them exceptionally well while I was away in California. In the midst of personal struggle, my Lord allowed me to experience my dream.

The boys performed above expectations and fought their way to the Arizona 2A State Championship. Amidst the wild celebration after the final game, Jill ran down the arena steps and whispered in my ear, "you did it."

I had the privilege of traveling the road with some incredible young men and coaches to the pinnacle. What a feeling. All the years of striving for that moment, and it was just what I dreamed it would be. But you know, it wasn't about self-worth, like I believed. What if we had lost? It was and always has been about the journey.

We were fortunate that time to win, but for my Lord it was all about the journey. It's all about His grace. In the midst of personal struggle and healing from years of pain I experienced great joy. That's what the healing journey is all about. In the middle of the storm, in the swirl of Satan's lies, you have to battle and fight for joy. Jesus doesn't set failure upon you. It is not his design to see you suffer or fail. Sin has a grip on this world, and circumstance after circumstance causes us to doubt his love and grace. My worth did not change the day the boys won the title. My worth has been the most important thing to Jesus from the day I was born. He is very fond of me.

The Lord of my heart has walked alongside all these years cheering me on, crying when I cry, and hurting when I hurt. He gave me—he gave all of us—the greatest gift of all: the ability to choose. The pain and the struggle from abuse is horrible. Jesus understands that. He suffered abuse of every kind on the cross. Jesus understands sin; it was my uncle's choice to abuse me, not Jesus'. The Lord wasn't just standing by allowing him to hurt me, He was standing by crying. Crying for my pain and crying for my uncle's choice to sin. It all plays out in the fallen creation; it is not what God wanted. But now, twelve years beyond the day I surrendered and opened my heart, I am learning to heal, I am learning to trust, I am experiencing the joy of my salvation. Choose to heal. Choose to hope. Fight for joy.

A few weeks after the state championship, I was reading in my office at home and a thought came to me. *Bill, why don't you share your story with Christian Schools?* I believe the Holy Spirit directs our thoughts, and I believe the Lord placed this one in my heart to say, it's time. There are millions that need to hear the words of hope that come through Jesus. I shared the idea with Jill, and we agreed. I researched all the issues necessary to form a nonprofit corporation, and in May of 2008 Holding on to Hope Ministries was born.

Think for a moment from whence I have come. Just twelve years earlier I was living two lives—one the world could see and one in utter darkness. For thirty years I had allowed Satan and my fears to shadow the grace and joy my Lord wanted for me. It was a measure of my faith and doubt in the power of Christ. It was sin against my wife and family. It was my weakness, it was my choice. But when I spoke up, when I chose to fight back, that was the moment the healing began.

Notice that it took twelve years to get to the moment where I could step out and trust. I started a ministry with no money, no experience, no contacts, and no resources. Someone who is afraid to fail would never make that move. But here I am, and once again, my Lord is walking alongside, cheering me on, crying when I cry, and telling everyone how fond He is of me.

Over the summer I scheduled speaking engagements at five Christian schools and seminars at five Christian school conventions. Funds and resources began to trickle in from faithful family and friends as we shared our vision to speak out for the broken. On September 30, 2008, I launched out and spoke at two Christian schools in Illinois. Two days later I shared three one-hour seminars on the nature and prevalence of abuse, and I shared my story. I had the opportunity to share the dream of hope with others. In my fifty-three years of church attendance, Christian school chapels, and thousands of services, I had never heard anyone share about abuse. What a moment, that my Lord prepared for me. "What some meant for evil, God meant for good."

Lest you think that Satan has surrendered; lest you think that life is about fairy-tale endings; lest you think the battle is over and I will live happily ever after—just three days after the wonderful convention I was at my daughter's home in Illinois. Without any warning whatsoever, I suffered a severe heart attack.

In my Lord's providence, Jill was with me on the trip (we rarely travel together). She is a Registered Nurse. My daughter lives in a small town, and the EMTs were at her house in minutes and transported me to the hospital in short order. A team of wonderful medical professionals was waiting and did everything necessary to save my life, including making arrangements to have me flown to Rockford, Illinois, where a cardiologist was waiting to perform immediate surgery. The quick response and available resources saved my life and my heart from serious damage.

Coincidence? Circumstances that will challenge the faith of a lifelong abuse survivor? Strong move by the enemy to win back lost ground? You bet. All I know is that I am still here. I am a great sinner and Christ is a great Savior. I have more time to share the good news that Jesus Christ loves me. And I am determined more than ever to share what He has done for me.

He is working in this broken world. He has the only answer for healing wounded souls, and He is very fond of me and you. If you have suffered the trauma of abuse, gather the courage to tell your story. Embrace the hope of joy. Live in the truth of His love for you. If God has spared you this experience, thank Him for His grace and reach out to the wounded with compassion and love. Keep holding on to the hope our Savior promises to all who love Him.

Conclusion

This book emphasizes the darkness and pain I have suffered from unwanted sexual abuse for over forty years now. I live with the damage every day; however, much of those forty years has been filled with times of joy, happiness, and celebration. The blessings of parenting my wonderful children, the satisfaction of accomplishments as a teacher and coach, and the joys of traveling the journey with the world's greatest partner. The Lord has granted me times of peace and joy and happiness that often overshadow the shattered past. Looking back over the years I see the truth of my Savior walking beside me and the grace He extended to me unaware.

My parents' strong commitment to the truth of God's Word, and their diligence in modeling for me the truth, established a foundation that enabled me to withstand the early abuse. While my parents were certainly not perfect, they were committed to each other and taught me the value of family security and the value of God's truth.

My children have been stalwart in their love and acceptance of me. All the years of being a dad, coaching, cheering, listening, and encouraging were also gifts of grace. I only wish I had told the children sooner why I behaved the way I did. I treasure their unconditional love and acceptance.

Joree has made an enormous impact on our family, and me in particular. While she is totally disabled, she can connect with anyone she meets with her infectious smile. Every morning I get her dressed, her smile beams and reminds me that I have so much to be grateful for. All these years as I have walked through the pain, she encourages me to press on. One day, Dad, we will walk together. My arms and legs will work the way our Lord designed, my tongue will sing. my wounded and broken body will be whole and my damaged soul will be healed. We will travel this healing road together, and we will encourage each other together until we walk together with the Savior of our lives.

Finally, I would not be where I am today without the perseverance, love, and commitment of the little blond girl I met when I was ten years old. Jill often says to me that God made her for me. All these years, through all the great times and certainly all the rough times, she has stood by me and walked ahead of me and through it all loved me beyond measure. I know lesser women may have left me, and rightly so, and yet she remained, supported, and held me through the journey. There is no greater gift than God's gift to me of my faithful angel.

Take courage, never give up, hold on to hope.

"Blessed is a man who perseveres under trial; for once he has been approved, he will receive the crown of life which the Lord has promised to those who love Him" (James 1:12).

Epilogue

Jillian's Story

W hen Bill asked me to write my own chapter, my immediate thought was, *I'm not the writer, you are.* Yet it was me who prayed that God would press on Bill's heart just how a book about his life could be a helpful tool to so many. I guess I never thought that my life alongside of Bill's could also be helpful. So with much prayer . . . this is my story.

Like all little girls, I dreamed of finding a tall, dark, and handsome man and having a beautiful, fairy-tale wedding. Growing up the middle child of five, I remember many happy moments. A big part of our family was singing. We were called the "Singing Sampsons." My mom played the piano, and along with my brothers and sisters we visited different churches on Sunday evenings, singing and sharing our faith. My parents taught us the truths of the Bible when we were very young, so it was natural for all of us to sing and share the message with many people. God was so good to allow me to be the daughter of Chuck and Hope Sampson's Christian heritage.

Bill was my tall, dark, and handsome man at my beautiful, fairy-tale wedding on August 30, 1975. We were married in our childhood church, where we met and ultimately fell in love. Our wedding day couldn't have been more perfect. We exchanged our original vows and embarked on a journey together with God and our family's blessings.

The weeks and months unfolded quickly. I always knew I talked more than Bill, but living with the day-to-day reality of it was an adjustment. I always thought talking was my gift and that God truly did make Bill and me for each other. After all, it is said opposites attract. But it did seem I was always pulling words out of him.

One week before our second anniversary God blessed us with our first child. Jaimee Colleen was born August 23, 1977, 5 lbs. 13 oz. I thought life couldn't be any better. My dream of having a little girl had quickly became a reality. I absolutely loved being a mom. Two years later Jeffrey William was born, November 14, 1979, 6 lbs. 2 oz. We had the perfect family, a boy for dad and a girl for me, two kids for both of us. We were truly blessed. Life progressed like it does for most young families. The responsibilities brought many joys and many challenges, but we were a busy, godly, happy family.

As I approached my thirtieth birthday I really desired one more child. Bill wasn't as sure as me, but on December 8, 1984, we were blessed with Julee Marie, 6 lbs. 8 oz. I was thrilled again. We had our complete family. We loved being parents and enjoyed our role as we taught our children the values we were taught by our parents.

As the years flew by, music became a big part of my life again. The girls joined me in doing many mother/daughter banquets around Chicago. Jaimee started singing with me when she was five years old. Julee started at two and a half. She always wanted to do everything like her big sister. The girls and I have many wonderful memories from those days. Today the girls continue singing; both are part of their respective church worship teams. It is a delight for me to see this unfold in the third generation.

While the girls and I were practicing and performing, Bill was busy with basketball and Jeff was right alongside him. Life as I knew it was pretty good, but let me fast forward a little bit.

We have all at one time or another in our life gone through sickness. We go to the doctor, we are diagnosed, we get antibiotics, and soon we are feeling much better. What if after a few days and all the medication you don't feel better?

The year was 1987. Life was grand. I was happily married to a wonderful man and had three wonderful children. Like everyone we were wrapped up in the crazy, busy, rat race schedule. Life was good — except for some persistent, painful and very annoying female problems. The symptom lingered for about a year. After a visit with the doctor, I was told that in order to have the pain and general fatigue go away, I would require a hysterectomy. Hmmm, I thought, okay, let's get this surgery over with so my happy busy life can continue on schedule. Being a nurse with a positive attitude, I knew I could have the surgery and bounce back and probably have even more energy than ever.

Bill and I talked with the kids and assured them that everything would be fine. I was admitted to Central DuPage. Hospital in June of 1988 for an abdominal hysterectomy. Everything seemed to be going fine until about 10 p.m. that night, when I started to hemorrhage. I was rushed into emergency surgery, and the outcome left me very, very sick. I remember thinking, *I'd rather be dead than have to deal with this pain.* Seven days later, following two blood transfusions and numerous pain medications, I was released from the hospital. But I was very weak. I wasn't sure if I would ever feel normal again.

The recovery was slow and exhausting, and I wrestled with God about my condition. "God, you have to give me back my strength. I have sooo much to do." I was working, I was a mom, a wife, an exercise instructor, my kids were in activities that needed me; I had singing engagements, my house needed my attention, I was a room mother, and on and on. God had another plan for me, and I was not even close to understanding or accepting it.

You would think that being a nurse I would know better, but I thought, *ah, just two weeks more; I will take it easy and I will be just like new.* That was my plan, or so I thought. Instead, it turned out to be the worst summer of my life. I relinquished some control and acknowledged that maybe God was trying to get my attention.

There I was, with zero energy. The more I tried, the more tired I became. My stubborn streak convinced me that in just five weeks I could return to work. I told myself that I could keep up no matter what. Instead, I suffered a physical, emotional, and spiritual breakdown over the next year. Do you think God was trying to get my attention?

I was now confined to bed eighteen to twenty hours a day. The condition lasted for almost two years. Now, all you moms and wives out there, think of what life would be like for your family in that situation. After months and months of tests and doctor visits, I was finally diagnosed with a fairly new autoimmune disease called Chronic Fatigue Syndrome and Fibromyalgia (which is like arthritis only it attacks your muscles). Unfortunately, there was no remedy at the time. My doctor's orders were to slow down your lifestyle, rest, and take medication. Do you think God was trying to get my attention?

Slowly I developed depression, mostly caused by the constant flu-like symptoms and inability to function. I maintained a low grade fever, every muscle in my body ached, I couldn't concentrate, I didn't care about anything or anyone, and all I wanted to do (and did) was cry. I felt guilty for not being able to function as a wife and mom. Additionally, it was during this time that the patient I had been caring for died. She was only thirty-eight years old. I was thirty-six years old, and remember one night telling Bill, very seriously, that it would be better for him and the kids if I would just die too. Wow, that scared Bill a lot. It was December of 1990.

Shortly thereafter, Bill took me to counsel with a psychiatrist. I thought I was just going to see another medical doctor. That day I started on antidepressant medication. You see, depression hit me like a brick because of the physical limitations the condition developed. Satan almost got a hold of me, but instead, God finally had my attention! God doesn't do random. If I truly believed in His Word, and I truly trusted Him, it was time to listen and try to understand exactly what He expected from me. God had to literally stop me completely so I would listen to His plan in my life. I was always so busy and full-speed ahead that I didn't take any time out to really listen to God.

Third John verse two (TLB) says, "Dear friend, I am praying that all is well with you and that your body is as healthy as I know your soul is." My soul is healthier now, and my body is functioning with some limitations. Sleep, medication, and warm weather all help me. In fact, it was the reason we moved to Arizona from Illinois. I praise God almost daily for bringing me to the desert. I still need reminders from my family about when to slow down, rest, and go average-speed ahead. But I am so thankful for the daily strength God allows me to have, because I know it is not mine alone.

I started back to work part-time in September 1991 and was assigned to a home of special needs foster children. They had a wide range of medical needs, but one special little girl there became my favorite. Her name was Jamie (of course, I liked that name, having a Jaimee of my own) but she had severe cerebral palsy. She couldn't feed herself, and in fact was primarily fed by a nasal gastric feeding tube. She was always smiling, and we quickly bonded.

Jamie was born at just twenty-seven weeks gestation, and at four months old was given up for adoption by her parents. During my time working at this special home, four different families showed an interest in adopting little Jaime until they realized just how severe she really was. They all said "no." It came to the point that they were going to place her in an institution, assuming she would probably die young.

Well, because of my special love for her, something inside of me thought—*why don't I bring her to our home and have our home be her foster home*. After a couple overnight visits and family discussions, we all overwhelmingly said, "YES."

When we moved to Arizona and applied for our state foster care license, it took over a year to process the paperwork. That is very normal. In Illinois we processed and received the license in just two weeks. From the beginning we have seen God's hand in all the processing and are reminded of His miraculous grace.

After a few days of baby Jamie and our Jaimee in the same house, we changed her name to Joree. That was 1992, and she has been with us ever since. She has brought more joy to our home than we ever imagined. Joree has an infectious smile that brightens everyone she meets. She has endured many hospital stays, and at eighteen years old continues to lighten up her world despite her inability to speak. Her smile and laugh are contagious. Yes, we've had to give up some things. The limits a wheelchair and special needs child place on you are substantial. But we feel as a family that she gives us much, much more than we could ever give her.

The reason I share all this about Joree with you is because I am convinced that if I had not gone through all my physical setbacks I would never have been accepting of having Joree be a part of my life and family. Joree was born January 17, 1991, right around the time I started to begin healing. God's timing is the best timing. God's plan was to make Joree a part of our family, and as of April 22, 1996, she legally became our daughter.

We are told that God knows what is best for our life. I am sure all of us can look back on an event or situation that at the time was devastating. Years later, though, we see it as God's complete plan, His best plan for our life. I Corinthians 13:12 (my paraphrase) says, "I know when I see Jesus face to face; I will understand totally every reason He allowed this in my life." Right now, looking back, I know it was God's only way to stop me and teach me to listen and learn to depend totally on Him. God allowed all of this for me. I could not always say that. Now, I say it and mean it from my heart. "Thank you, God, for allowing the trials in my life to grow and strengthen my love and trust in you."

Little did I know that through this trial and healing that an even tougher one was just around the corner. As Joree became such a big part of our family and continued to be part of my healing, she in fact was becoming part of a bigger healing, for my dear husband, Bill. In sharing this next part of the story, my hope and prayer is that it will help someone else, if even in a small way.

Around the time I began to feel a little normal again, things between Bill and I began to breakdown. The stress and communication issues between us seemed to only worsen with each passing week. With everything I tried, I still could not understand his moodiness and days of silence. After several suggestions to Bill that maybe seeing a counselor could help us, he just replied with the same "no" with complete emptiness in his eyes.

I really was not sure what to do next. His mood swings were not only affecting me, but our children as well. I felt I couldn't make any more excuses for him to the children because I truly didn't understand it myself. Jaimee was eighteen, Jeff sixteen, Julee eleven, and Joree four. God was such a strong part of our family; it just did not make sense.

Not long after, Bill met me for lunch when he was principal of Aurora Christian School. I did not realize it at the time, but our world was about to be flipped upside down with the heartfelt words Bill tearfully shared with me. It is hard to explain, but I felt God's peace and comfort along with almost unspeakable shock, as I listened to him speak so emotionally. Bill shared with me how at age thirteen a trusted family member on visits to his parent's home sexually abused him. I remember thinking to myself, "How in the world was this innocent young boy able to take all this new and confusing emotion and be able to discern what was happening?"

The abuse continued, and he was told to never speak of this "special connection" to anyone, especially his parents. As I listened, my heart and soul were screaming out with intense anger, and yet wanting to hug and comfort Bill at the same time. Here we were, sitting in a restaurant, and I was hearing how thirty years earlier my husband of twenty years was abused over and over and over again. We both felt the heavy emotion of it all, and the tears kept flowing.

Over the next few days and weeks, my questions as to how and why increased. I slowly began to understand reasons for Bill's moodiness, hours of silence, and his ever-changing personality traits. I continued to realize little by little just how much damage this horrible abuse brought to my husband's entire life. I saw how it affected every person he came in contact with, every choice that was given to him, every decision he had to make, and every emotion that faced him. His entire personality and ability to interact with others was deeply wounded. Our journey of healing after that first conversation moved very, very slowly.

As Bill's wife, what was I going to do to help him? How and where should we begin this difficult walk? My mind went in circles and my heart raced, and I felt like I could hardly breathe. These thoughts and verses came to me as if God came down and spoke them directly into my ear. *Marriage is not about perfection, it is about unity, blending strengths and forgiving weaknesses to become together what neither could alone* (see I Peter 3:1-7).

I am a nurse and a middle child, and have always been and continue to be the person who thinks I can fix everything. So I went into fix mode. First, send a certified letter to the abuser and let him know his secret was finally out after thirty years of silence. That helped me deal with my anger for the moment. Second, tell Bill's mom so the love, comfort, and compassion that all children need from their mother will be communicated through love and forgiveness. Of course, I didn't foresee how difficult this process would be for both of them, but I truly felt it was a needed step for Bill's healing. My primary thoughts were always, *I need to fix this problem for everyone so Bill does not continue to have this heavy burden and shame follow him through our lives.* I wanted the dark days to be over for him as quickly as possible.

Third, get us both to a Christian counselor. I discovered I needed just as much help as Bill did in knowing the best way of dealing with this situation. We met with a recommended counselor, but things did not go well. Bill revolted against the counselor and his methods and took it out on me and the children. It took over six years to return to a point where Bill was ready to confront the past again.

It was 2004, and we had settled into another routine—only this time in Phoenix, Arizona. Bill took a job at Northwest Christian School as administrator. The move was positive, but after six years our life together had once again deteriorated to the breaking point. I arranged to meet a highly recommended Christian counselor without informing Bill, and when he arrived home from school, I proceeded to tell him that we would be leaving immediately. . I stated that if we were going to make our life together work, he must come with me. I continued to tell him that I would be going with or without him, because I needed help for myself as much as he needed it for himself.

With some very strong resistance he decided to go. He was in the car physically, but was obviously not there mentally. The two hour drive was total dead silence. After all, if I didn't talk, there would be no conversation at all, which was the norm. What Bill didn't know was that I was silently and urgently praying to God the entire way.

When we arrived, Bill's anger only continued to build. I just kept praying. The next few hours spent with Patti, the counselor, were a real tug-of-war with God and Satan. It was getting quite late, and it was obvious that Bill was threatening to leave. I stated again that I was staying the night and would work with Patti again the next day as we had planned. Bill was really angry at me, Patti, and God. Then she challenged him to take a book with him and that she would make sure I got home on Sunday.

I went to bed still praying. Bill never came in. I knew he didn't leave and figured he was sleeping on the couch in the other room. It was a restless night to say the least. When I awoke, I realized that Bill had in fact stayed up all night. He had read the entire book that Patti challenged him with and was very touched and ready to talk. God was working. We spent the day walking with him through the past, the memories, and the pain. Many, many tears were shed that day, but we left knowing we had God and each other to help us through the journey ahead.

Finally, the fourth step that was critical for us was sharing the story with the children. It was difficult for them to understand or relate to the pain their father had endured. Yet each of them sensed as they grew up that there was something about Dad that was mysterious. They weren't sure what it was, but they sensed it. Upon hearing the story, their hearts reached out in a new way to Bill that was genuine, loving, and supportive. We can't go back and fix those days for them.

Their unconditional love for their father has been a blessing and healing potion for both of us.

This journey we all travel is filled with surprises every day. I lived with the man of my dreams for twenty years without ever knowing he held inside a deep, dark secret. We are thirteen years down the road from that moment. No one ever said this journey would be easy, and it hasn't been. It's all about trusting in Jesus, the Savior of our soul. His faithfulness is new every morning.

The Israelites passed on to their children and grandchildren stories of what God had done and would do in their lives so that they would know the Lord and love and worship him. If God is working mightily in our lives, what benefit is there from keeping it to ourselves? We need to share our trials, tribulations, and triumphs with those who will live beyond us. For it is the only way the next generation will know of our love for our Lord.

It wasn't until Bill included me in the journey that he was able to begin healing. I know he would tell any victim of abuse, you have to tell your story. Don't keep it inside; share it with someone you love and the world. It isn't easy, but it is truly the way to hope.

When I reflect back over our marriage and see just how far God has brought us, I am overwhelmed with gratitude. Did I do the best I could? Let's just say, "I'm still working on it."

My Children's View

I asked my children to answer several questions regarding their growing up years and how they perceived my behaviors. As you read you will understand why I am among men, most blessed. Despite my shortcomings God's grace has granted me the greatest children in the world. They have never waivered in their love for me and every day they lift and encourage my heart to persevere. They are committed to serving their Lord and Savior. There is no greater gift for Jillian and I than to have them in our lives. Let their words encourage you.

Jaimee and her husband Jason have two children, Jakob and Jaylin. They are committed to serving our Lord and minister as worship leaders in their local church.

Jeffrey and his wife Alanna have two children as well, Payson and Lola. Jeff is a successful business man and together they serve as lay workers in their local church.

Julee and her husband Ryan serve as well in their local church. They work as teachers in the local public high school Julee is a special education teacher and coach and one day they look forward to having children of their own.

Joree, our youngest daughter cannot speak for herself. If she could, I believe she would tell you that Jesus loves you. Hold on to that hope.

What was it like growing up with dad?

Jaimee:

I must say that overall, growing up with dad was a wonderful experience. It helped mold me into who I am today. I always had a respect for my dad. I looked up to him and often desired his advice. I didn't feel my dad was absent or uninvolved overall. It wasn't until I was older that I was able to pinpoint and understand how his silence on many issues affected me. There came moments in my life when I really wanted to know what he was thinking but developed a fear of asking…I guess a fear more of silence. He wasn't one to explode, yell, or become overbearing, in fact, he was a great listener. He weighed everything out before responding which is why I asked for his advice. The hard part was the times you didn't receive a response. Without knowing it, I was learning a behavior that was a result of his abuse (lack of trust, silence, etc.). Even though I was not sexually abused like my dad, I modeled the behavior of someone who was abused. This does not excuse the sin aspect of that behavior in my life. It is only through Christ that I can overcome those behaviors. I don't blame my dad for different personality traits and behaviors I have learned. God places the people (including our parents) in our lives, and vice versa, to mold us into becoming more like Him. I hope to embrace Christ in all my faults, failures, idiosyncrasies, learned behaviors, experiences (good and bad), in order to become more like Him. God is sovereign over all things; I thank God for the earthly father he gave me. He loves God, his wife, and his children. He modeled Christ the best he knew how and helped point me to the heavenly Father. When all is said and done, that is all that will matter anyway.

Jeffrey:

It's strange answering this question today because looking back I now know what happened, but at the time dad was just dad. It seemed at times he had multiple personalities. We would have an absolute blast on a vacation or outing where dad would be completely positive and cheery and then you might have a time where he stormed out of the room after a discussion and you were left asking yourself, "What was that"?

A classic example was during my career as a basketball player. Dad had been coaching my entire life and was my coach in high school. Basketball was a huge part of both of our lives so naturally there were many discussions and situations that involved the sport. He was my coach pretty much throughout my career and I at times felt like I needed to coach and encourage him. For example no matter how good our team played it always seemed that I had to build up his confidence as he was always quick to go negative and assume there was no way we could defeat whomever the next team we were playing.

I learned at a very young age that it never seemed that I would ever measure up completely or be good enough to "make it" to some future level. As a kid I dreamed of playing at a high level which started in fourth and fifth grades. Because of being around the game at a very young age I was leaps and bounds ahead of other players and would essentially score 25 of our 28 team points. As I got older and kids got bigger coupled with what I perceived as negative comments I realized I may not make it and accepted it. Later when I was enlightened about my dad's abuse it dawned on me that some of the damage he suffered and his behavior trickled down to me. As I grew I just realized that it was not really my dream anyway despite believing I would have been capable of playing at the next level.

Julee:

Being the youngest of the three kids and so distant in age from my older siblings, I believe my perspective may be a bit different. As far as I was concerned, I had a completely functional family. I had many wonderful memories from my childhood with my dad. I was an incredibly active kid who loved sports and since my dad was a college basketball coach he would often take me with him to work. I formed a unique bond with my dad at a young age. I believe basketball played a large role in this bond. Again, because I was so much younger than my brother and sister, I required more attention and dad and I would often go on bike rides, out for ice-cream, shoot hoops or play catch.

One part of growing up with dad that I always thought was unusual was that he left the disciplining to my mom. I can remember one time at a very young age my dad spanked me. I remember this clearly because I did not cry as result of the pain, but from the fact that my dad was the one who did it. He immediately hugged me and said he was sorry and a tear ran down his face. That was the first and last time he would ever spank me. Little did I know at the time the purpose of this behavior.

When I was a bit older there were times that I could remember dad's unusual moods. He would be very quiet and distant. Sometimes he would snap at us if we were bothering him. I never understood the sadness that would come over him and it made it very difficult to talk with him; but we always knew not to bother him and that the mood would eventually pass. The older I got the more observant I would become and distance began to come between dad and I.

I could not have asked for a better childhood and I never once questioned my dad's love for me. He was affectionate, encouraging and always pushed me to do the best I could and never quit. He showed us how to live for Jesus Christ and always put him first and for that I am forever grateful.

How did you perceive dad's behavior changes?

Jaimee:

Since dad has shared his story, I have seen a huge burden lifted. He can openly talk about his past (without detail of course) without figuring out new ways to hide it. On the other hand, there have been some very dark times as well. The weight of the sin was lifted in one sense, but the pain of going back to the memories and dealing with it again was very difficult. Satan does not want his story to be used for good. In order to share his story, some dark sins are revealed and remind him and others of how decrepit our sin nature really is. The issue of sexual abuse is not a light one, no matter how discreet you are about it. It affects people of all ages in the core of their very being. It is heart-wrenching to think that the human heart is so depraved.

Jeffrey:

When I found out about dad's abuse it most definitely "cleared" things up. I was 17 years old at the time, which looking back was a good age. Prior to that you are really just a kid and may not be able to truly grasp the ramifications of what had happened. It definitely took some time to soak in. My initial response was anger and sadness for dad. But, as I reflected and began to mesh the abuse with memories I began to understand more and more his behavior. I have since realized what great courage it took to sit down and tell your 17 year old son what happened and I am proud of what he is doing today as he strives to serve God through his sharing his past.

Julee:

I am not sure if changed my impression as much as confirmed my suspicion about his behavior. When we moved to Arizona, I was going into high school and was for the most part an only child. My dad was my teacher, principal and basketball coach; needless to say, it was hard to avoid him. With all of this time spent with him I was able to observe his behavior frequently. I always knew there had to be something that happened to him in his life that he was keeping from us, but I could never ask. I was devoted to praying for my dad. I did not always know why I was praying but I always felt led to do so.

When I was a freshman in college, the information about his past was revealed and the burden was lifted from my dad, I too felt relieved to finally have an explanation for the behavior. I immediately began thanking the Lord because I saw this as an answer to prayer that I had for so long been looking for. Little did I know the challenges that were to come for our family.

What did you think when you found out about his past? Did it change your view or impression of him in any way?

Jaimee:

The initial response was shock and a variety of mixed emotions. I was angry, sad, confused, embarrassed, compassionate, etc. So many questions filled my mind. Many of them were questions that my dad feared we would ask if we found out. I wanted the abuser to die at first! Then I learned he was already dead. I wanted to know if any of it was my dad's fault. I wanted to be there for my dad as if he was a little boy again. I wanted to somehow save him from the treacherous acts. The question of "why" was there as well. Did he have any diseases? Why did God allow that? Why did his mom not stop that? How could a "trusted" relative use the innocence/ignorance of a child? I can't even sum up the thoughts and questions that raced through my mind as I bawled in my husband's arms after hearing.

Of course it changed my view or impression. It gave me a new perspective on so many traits my dad obtained. The "secret" was put on the table for all to see! It didn't even happen to me and yet there was a part of me that wanted to hide it too! However, it was freeing at the same time. The freedom to understand my dad in a new way was opening a door to healing. We were able to discuss issues in a new light! We were dealing with the depth of issues...not just the surface. We saw what was underneath and that lead to healing for all of us in some way. I must note: It didn't make me love him less. I think that fear of being exposed is really a fear of not being loved or wanted. I hope that my dad experienced the love and acceptance from his family more than he could have ever imagined. God brings the secret sins to light to be exposed for healing. He can do a much greater work in those that confess and repent as opposed to those who hid in the darkness their whole life. I have seen that is an awful place to be and ultimately, Christ's love is shown greater in weakness than in a "strong, put-together" person with "no problems or secrets".

Jeffrey:
For me, dad's behavior changes were just dad. We all learned if he was not talking or in one of his "moods" just to leave him alone and fend for ourselves if we needed something. At times it was extremely frustrating because you just wanted to be able to sit down and ask advice about a certain situation but you knew that wasn't an option because it would just be hollow. After I learned of the abuse I suppose I was more sympathetic and would not necessarily give up and would push him hoping it would help.

Julee:
Because I was with my dad so much in high school, I perceived the behavior changes as stress related because he

was a principal. I also saw my dad as somewhat of a perfectionist and if he would fail at a task he would get very down on himself. All of these scenarios would trigger a mood and from my point of view that was the extent. Although this is true, I did not realize that this was only scratching the surface and the reason for the behavior was much deeper.

Do you think your dad's abusive past now affects the way you parent your children?

Jaimee:

I would like to start by saying I never want to blame my parents for who I am or what I've become. There are ways that we learn from our imperfect parents that we pass on to our children. We are all imperfect in a fallen world. I will pass on imperfections and sinful personality traits to my children. As sad as that is, those of us with Christ are striving each day to live like Him and for Him as we model Jesus to our children. He is molding us as we "mold" our children.

Okay, with that said, I have definitely picked up a "lack of trust" factor in my life that could be just the way I am, or learned to some extent from my dad's speculative demeanor. He has always tended to be very careful with trusting people's motives. I suppose I have adopted that and imposed it on my children. I am careful to a fault I guess, always questioning who has my children. I have had to let the fear of them being abused go in certain cases. I am thankful God has given me discernment and wisdom. I am growing in allowing God to protect them in many areas. I can be wise and somewhat cautious, but not fearful. I think my parents did a good job with parenting and disciplining us. My dad did mention once, after we found out about the abuse, that he had a hard time spanking us or raising his voice often because he felt somehow he was hurting us. I don't feel that, so when it comes to parenting, I don't share the same feelings or regrets he does or did.

Jeffrey:

I would say it does to some degree. Even knowing that dad's behavior was a product of abuse I still spent so many years under his leadership that it definitely affected who I am. The great thing about knowing about the abuse is that I can recognize similar behaviors during or after I am emulating them. I tend to withdraw sometimes if things get a little chaotic, which anyone who has three and two year old knows can happen. Most of the time I catch myself right away, ask for Gods patience and strength, and do my best to push through. I thank God often that Dad had the courage to come forward because if he hadn't I would most likely not understand the behavior and its root.

I would encourage anyone who has not told there children and if they are at an age they would be able to understand that they tell them. I have more respect for my dad for telling us as opposed to if he had not told us and we found out later in life.

Julee:

Because my husband Ryan and I have yet to be blessed with children, we often talk about how we would like to raise them. I often think about how my dad's negative behavior has affected my own behavior and how I have practiced this behavior in my own life. I pray daily that the Lord would do a work in me to overcome this behavior and mold me to be more like Christ as I do not want the negativity to impact my own children someday. I was not aware of the affect my dad's behavior had on me until my husband began to point it out in me. This is one area specifically that I will continue to pray that the Lord will make me an example of Christ for my children so they can mature into Christlike examples.

What advice would you give others who may be in a similar situation?

Jaimee:

As far as advice for a child to a parent who has been abused, love them unconditionally as Christ would. If you're confused or doubting, or just need some answers, communicate it to them in love. If some of the behaviors have become some of your own behaviors, seek help and seek Christ to heal you as well! It may not look the same as your parent, but it still needs help and healing.

As for advice to the parent? Love your child unconditionally. You have taken a bold and brave step in sharing your past to help you and them move on and grow in Christ. I would also advise not to disclose too many details. That doesn't help the child heal, it only creates questions that aren't necessary for them to know or dwell on. Even though it helps the child to understand where you're coming from, it doesn't help them to think on the sin or darkness that has taken place.

Jeffrey:

Talk about it, pray about it and trust God to bring you through it. As all things in life it will be a journey. It won't be easy but together with God's help you will progress and healing will take place. What I have come to realize is that abused or not abused we are all broken wounded sinners who need Jesus to stand before the Lord on our own behalf. My goal is to become more like Christ at the end than I was at the beginning. Yes, the journey of life flows up and down. You have good seasons and bad seasons. But, unless you rely on Christ to stay at the foot of the cross you won't make it. I am telling you, it ain't happening without Him!

I am proud and have great respect for dad's desire to finish strong and use the abuse in his life to help the healing process for others. I can honestly say that he has been an inspiration for me and helped me strive to be a better man and father. I love you dad!

Julee:

First I would say that overcoming such a horrible situation would not be possible without the love and grace of my Lord and Savior Jesus Christ. It is only by his love and grace that my dad and family have been given hope for the future. When my dad hit rock bottom, it seemed like he would never get through, but thanks be to Christ he overcame and continues to heal by the grace of God. I also would say to never cease to pray. When times would seem tough, I would get on my knees and pray sometimes for hours. It was these times that I felt God's presence the most and I could see a work being done in my family. Faith can be very difficult for many people to grasp, but I believe it in situations like these that an individual's faith is strengthened. Hold on to the love of Christ because he is our hope for the future.